# The Turkey Hunter's Bible

# The Turkey Hunter's Bible

## John E. Phillips

D O U B L E D A Y

NEW YORK  TORONTO  LONDON  SYDNEY  AUCKLAND

PUBLISHED BY DOUBLEDAY
a division of Bantam Doubleday Dell Publishing Group, Inc.
666 Fifth Avenue, New York, New York 10103

DOUBLEDAY are the portrayal of an anchor with a dolphin
are registered trademarks of Doubleday, a division of Bantam
Doubleday Dell Publishing Group, Inc.

Library of Congress Cataloging-in-Publication Data

Phillips, John E.
    The turkey hunter's bible / John E. Phillips. — 1st ed.
        p.    cm.
    1.  Turkey hunting.    I.  Title.
SK325.T8P486    1992
799.2'48619 — dc20                    92-25084
                                               CIP
ISBN: 0-385-42223-7

November 1992

FIRST EDITION

To my sister, Betty Sue Jackson.
Thanks, Sis.

# Contents

# Acknowledgments

Writing this book required many hands and long hours by devoted people who believed in the project.

I want to thank Carol Evans, who greeted each day with a headset telephone and a computer, and who typed and researched diligently until the manuscript was completed. John P. Lee, of Montevallo, Alabama, one of the nation's best wildlife illustrators, met stringent deadlines to provide the illustrations found in these pages.

Denise Phillips, Marjolyn McLellan, Margaret Smith, Cara Clark, Elizabeth Tittle and Kirsten Hunt all participated in typing and organizing the manuscript. Henry Gross's masterful editing and production skills helped make the book what it is. Also, special thanks to John Duff of Doubleday, who believed enough in the project to commission it.

Without the support, help, inspiration, and encouragement of all these people and others, this book would not have been possible.

# Preface

For more than thirty years, the love call of the sultan of the dogwoods has lured me out of my bed and into the turkey woods long before daylight only to be made a fool of more often than I have been victorious.

I believe the wild turkey should be the symbol of America rather than the scavenger bald eagle. The turkey is crafty and intelligent and survives because of his keen instincts. His only Achilles tendon is his passionate desire once a year for every hen he can find. Some smart gobblers have learned to sublimate their sex drives for the sake of survival, reaching the status of legends to the men who hunt them.

For me, there's no finer or richer moment than when the bronze baron of the long beard and the sharp spurs flexes his muscles, displays his manhood and calls all hens to pay him homage. Only when the wild turkey gobbler abandons his habit of calling the hens to him and instead chases after them does he walk into harm's way and my gunsights.

This book is a tribute to all the gobblers that have outsmarted me and taught me the lessons found herein.

# 1

# The Wild Turkey

Before Christopher Columbus landed on the banks of the New World, the Indians were hunting and domesticating the wild turkey. They called to turkeys, flushed them, ran them with dogs and horses, shot them on their roosts, trapped them in trenches by baiting and then shot them with bow and arrow.

The ancestral range of the turkeys living on our continent in the early days included an area of about forty states. The Indians of what would become Virginia and North Carolina, as well as the Aztecs of Mexico, farmed and raised wild turkeys.

Evidence suggests the wild turkey and the domesticated turkey were both important foods for the Indian. Indians not only ate turkeys but also used them for decoration, clothing, sewing and ceremonial items. The Crows, a Rocky Mountain tribe, used the leg bones of turkeys to make ceremonial whistles, which were highly prized possessions. Prehistoric pottery of the Mexican Indians—both petroglyphs (rock pickings) and pictographs (paintings)—showed turkey images.

Cortez probably took the Mexican turkey back to Spain around 1519, where it was domesticated and spread across Europe, later returning to North America with the Pilgrims in the 1600s. An estimated 10 million turkeys lived in the New World when the first permanent colony was established at Plymouth, Massachusetts, in 1620. Early settlers brought caged specimens of domestic turkeys with them but still preferred the meat of the wild turkey. The diaries of these colonists often mentioned flocks of more than 5,000 turkeys.

By the 1800s, market hunting for wild turkey had became popular. Commercial hunters tried to develop ways to take the greatest amount of meat using the least amount of powder, shot and effort. Among their tactics for taking turkeys was "lining." A trail of corn was laid out in a straight line as bait. Turkeys would crowd shoulder to shoulder along the line with their heads down, eating the corn. The hunters would call to them, the turkeys would raise their heads to investigate, and the hunters would pick them off.

In the 1800s, the thought of protecting the turkey was unheard of and seemed ridiculous

A camouflaged hunter comes face to face with a wild turkey he called into range.
With intelligent management, the bird has made a remarkable comeback.

and unnecessary since the supply seemed inexhaustible. From the 1860s until the early 1900s, market hunting was at its height. As a consequence, the turkey was gone from Connecticut by 1813, from Massachusetts by 1851, from Ohio by 1880 and from Michigan by 1881. By the end of World War II, what originally had been a population of 10 million or more turkeys had been reduced to only 30,000 birds in the entire United States.

In the early 1900s, President Theodore Roosevelt, a dedicated outdoorsman and conservationist, asked Congress to set aside wildlife refuges and begin a planned, scientific way to help America's dwindling wildlife. However, it wasn't until 1935 that the Cooperative Wildlife Research Unit Program was established. Then in 1937 Congress passed the Federal Aid to Wildlife Restoration Act, the Pittman-Robertson Act, which legislated a hunter tax and thereby directly aided the American turkey. Hunters paid a tax on guns and equipment, and this money was used to aid wildlife and wildlife restoration. This act, along with increased knowledge and awareness of the plight of the wild turkey, helped the turkey to come back.

By 1958, the turkey population had increased through restocking and protection so that the birds could be hunted in many parts of the United States, although in sections of Alabama, Louisiana and some other southern states, turkey season never had been closed. Now the wild turkey is present in fifty states and in Canada and Mexico.

Support, protection and conservation of the wild turkey continues. The National Wild Turkey Federation (NWTF) was incorporated in 1973 as a nonprofit conservation and education organization. The NWTF established a Research Foundation in 1981 to solicit funds and use these for wild turkey research nationwide. In 1986, the NWTF and the U.S. Forest Service signed an agreement to provide money and volunteers to maintain and improve wild turkey habitat and conduct research on Forest System lands. By 1988, the national flock of wild turkeys was at one-fifth of its original

Early market hunters laid a trail of corn to bait turkeys into a line so they presented an easy target. Then they picked them off one by one.

In the late 19th century, market hunting had reached its height in the United States and the turkey population rapidly declined.

number. Today a conservative estimate puts the turkey population at 3.5 million.

## PHYSICAL DESCRIPTION

An average adult male turkey stands about 4 feet tall and weighs from 15 to 20 pounds. It has brilliantly colored plumes of metallic green, copper and bronze. Body feathers have black tips, and a tuft of bristle-like feathers called a beard hang from the male's breast. Turkey feathers insulate and cover. Their down feathers, which are closest to their bodies, are covered and shielded by vein feathers or contour feathers. The male bird also has spurs on his legs.

The head and the neck of the male turkey are featherless. A tom's head can be many col-

ors—purple, blue, white and/or red—depending on the gobbler's mood, the amount of blood flow or lack of it near the surface, the time of the year and the bird's home range. The growth on the front of the head is called a *snood* or a *dewbill*. The pouchlike area at the front of his throat, called a *wattle*, usually is the penetration target for the hunter. Small, fleshy, reddish growths of skin at the base of the throat are called *caruncles*.

The hen is smaller than the tom. Like most species of birds, the hen appears duller in color and has fewer if any bristles on the breast.

All turkeys are good runners, even when melting snow covers the ground. Audubon once followed a flock of running wild turkeys on horseback without being able to overtake them. However, one advantage hunters have is that these birds are poor fliers—except for

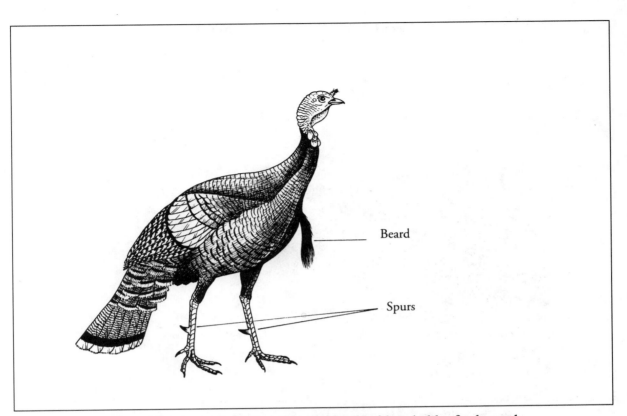

The turkey's beard is made of a tough tuft of bristle-like feathers; the male birds have spurs on their legs. On the turkey's head are the snood, the wattles and the caruncles.

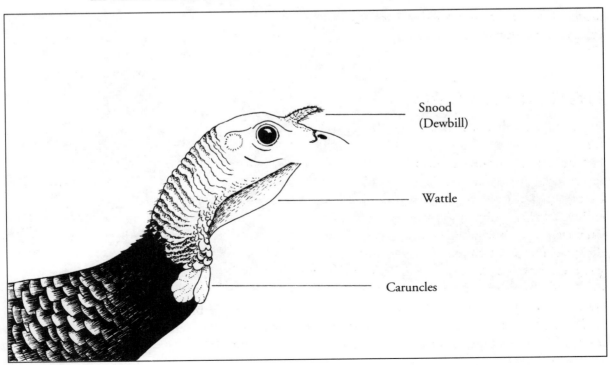

This eastern gobbler was taken by a hunter with a blackpowder muzzleloading shotgun, the same weapon used by early frontiersmen hunting their favorite quarry.

short distances—because they lack blood vessels in their breast muscles.

## SPECIES AND SUBSPECIES OF TURKEYS

There are two living species of turkeys—the turkey of North America *(Meleagris gallopavo)* and the smaller and more colorful ocellated turkey *(Meleagris ocellata)* of southern Mexico and Central America. Turkeys may have received their common name in any one of several ways. Some people think the Indian name for the bird, which was *furkee* or *firkee*, may have been changed in pronunciation to turkey. Others believe the North American turkey's scientific names, *Meleagris*, which means guineafowl, and *gallopavo*, which is derived from *gallus* (cock) and *pavo* (peafowl), support a theory that the turkey was confused with the guineafowl *(Nunida meleagris)* at one time. Since the guineafowl was thought to have originated in the country of Turkey, perhaps that is why the turkey was so named.

There are five subspecies of the wild turkey *(Meleagris gallopavo)*: the eastern, the Osceola, the Merriam and the Rio Grande of the United States and the Gould, of Mexico. The Mexican turkey, which is now extinct, was the ancestor of our domesticated birds. Many of the characteristics that identify the different subspecies are subtle and mostly limited to differences in gradations of color.

### Eastern Turkey

The eastern wild turkey *(Meleagris gallopavo silvestris)* has been restocked successfully across much of the United States. This turkey of the East, some parts of the Midwest and the South inhabits mainly farmlands and hardwood forests, an area that produces abundant mast crops. The species designator, *silvestris*, means woodlands. Pennsylvania, New York, Missouri and many of the southern states have large numbers of easterns, and Missouri is known nationwide for its vast turkey hunting opportunities. According to the NWTF, the record eastern wild turkey weighed 33¼ pounds, and the record atypical turkey had seven beards and 183.75 points. Many sportsmen believe the eastern wild turkey is the most difficult type to take.

Distinctive in appearance, the eastern turkey's tail tips can be chocolate color or buff. The primary wing feathers are barred with white divided by a black bar of similar width.

### Rio Grande Turkey

This gobbler, *Meleagris gallopavo intermedia*, is found throughout the arid Southwest. Texas, Oklahoma and California have the largest birds. Texas probably has the most. Rio Grandes also are found in Kansas, New Mexico and Mexico.

The Rio Grande looks much like a combination of the eastern and western strains, which probably is the reason for the subspecies Latin name, *intermedia*. The tail tips of this turkey can range from yellowish-buff in color to nearly pure white. The tail feather tips are almost always lighter than those of the eastern or the Osceola and are darker than the Merriam or the Gould.

The home of the Rio Grande ranges from the mesquite-dotted rangelands of Texas to the eastern-looking Kansas habitats with alternating farmland and hardwood ridges. Oklahoma's habitat is open farmland by tree-lined waterways. Obviously, the Rio Grande wild turkey is very adaptable. Because of the lack of foliage in this region, finding a good place to hide and to take a stand is especially difficult.

**The Rio Grande gobbler is found mainly in the deserts of Texas and throughout the Southeast.**

## Merriam Turkey

The Merriam turkey (*Meleagris gallopavo merriami*) is found in a wide range that includes South Dakota, California, Washington, Colorado, Minnesota, New Mexico, Nebraska and Wyoming. This bird originally lived in the mountainous areas of Arizona and New Mexico,

**The Merriam gobbler inhabits the high hill country of the West.**

but restocking has greatly increased its range.

The Merriam, named to honor zoologist C. Hart Merriam, is sometimes called the mountain turkey because much of its range is the ponderosa pine belt to the foothills that surround the mountains. The Merriam is a migratory turkey in some areas. Summer birds stay high on the mountains to take advantage of the pine tree roosts, cooler air and a better water and food supply. When snow falls, these turkeys move to the foothills that support transition woodlands. Biologists have estimated the trip between a Merriam's summer and winter habitats may be as far as sixty miles. Because of the high altitude at which the bird lives a hunter must be in top-notch physical condition.

Merriams look much like the other sub-species of turkeys, only their tail feathers are much whiter.

## Osceola Turkey

Because this subspecies, *Meleagris gallopavo osceola*, is found in the peninsula of Florida, it sometimes is called the Florida turkey. Other regions of Florida have wild turkeys, but they are either easterns or hybrids of the easterns and the Osceolas. The Osceola has the most restricted range of all the subspecies.

The Osceola bears the name of a 19th century Seminole chief who was undefeated in his war against the Americans. Because of the swamps, mosquitoes and rugged terrain of Florida, the Seminole nation was unconquered.

To take an Osceola gobbler, hunters have to face these same hazards as well as near tropical heat. The Osceola resembles the eastern turkey in coloration, but its body is smaller. Also, the barring of the wing feathers is slightly different, being predominantly black.

## Gould Turkey

This turkey, *Meleagris gallopavo mexicana,* is found predominantly in the northern range of Mexico in the Sierra Madre, although small groups also live in the area where New Mexico, Arizona and Mexico meet. State and federal game management officials hope these birds can come back to a good number in this part of their historic range, since the estimated Gould population in the U.S. was only 150 birds in 1989.

To make this hope a reality, the Arizona

**The Osceola gobbler, named after the famous war chief of the Seminole Indians, is also known as the Florida turkey.**

Game and Fish Department, the USDA Forest Service, the Bureau of Land Management, the U.S. Fish and Wildlife Service, the state and federal governments of Mexico, the Southeastern Cooperative Wildlife Disease Study of Athens, Georgia, and the NWTF have worked together to trap Gould turkeys in Mexico and have moved them into the Galiuro Mountains, a wilderness area in the Coronado National Forest.

The Gould turkey also migrates between a summer and a winter range. This bird resembles the Merriam gobbler in that the tips of its tail feathers are white but not as intense. The wide band that borders the tail feathers is wider than in the Merriam, and the rump patch usually is slightly smaller.

### Ocellated Turkey

The ocellated turkey, *(Meleagris ocellata)*, is a separate species rather than a subspecies. These birds are found on the Yucatan Peninsula of Mexico and in the adjoining Central American countries of Guatemala and Belize. The ocellata is a jungle bird.

Male and female ocellatas are similarly colored with an iridescent green body with gold, copper, bronze and red flashes of light. The ocellated turkeys have been called the most beautiful birds in the world. Interestingly, neither sex has a beard, but the males do have spurs. This bird is smaller than the gallopavo, and males average around 12 pounds, while some have reached 18 pounds.

## NATURAL HISTORY

The wild turkey's ability to live and multiply in the face of encroaching civilization is due to his keen senses of hearing and eyesight, and his ability ...

* To run at 12½ miles an hour.

* To cover a vast amount of ground by walking an average of 30,000 steps a day.
* To take off from the ground like a helicopter.
* To fly as fast as the speed limit on highways for short distances.
* To negotiate flight paths through trees.

The wild turkey feeds on nuts, seeds, insects, berries and other small fruits and animals, eating more than 354 species of plants and 313 kinds of small animals. A turkey can eat up to a pound of food per meal with its powerful gizzard that can crush the hardest foods. In snow, the turkey can scratch up to a foot deep to find food.

Wild turkeys, which gather in small flocks, are led in the spring by a dominant male known as a gobbler or a tom, which often has a harem of female hens. A definite pecking order is established within the flock. When the dominant male turkey is killed, another tom moves up to the dominant position in the pecking order.

The wild turkey's mating and reproductive systems make it particularly strong and disease-resistant. Usually only the dominant gobbler breeds. The hens lay a great number of eggs with only a few infertile. Gobblers prepare for mating season by feeding heavily and then living on their breast sponges—masses of thick, cellular tissue—during mating season when they do not have to take time to eat. If a hen's eggs or nest, which is built on the ground, are destroyed, and she then mates with a bird other than the dominant gobbler, a large proportion of the eggs will not develop.

Hens do the nesting. They are aggressive in protecting the nests from all predators—including raccoons, skunks, and foxes. Coyotes, particularly, have become a problem in many parts of the country. Turkey eggs, which are almost twice the size of chicken eggs, are a pale creamy-tan with brown speckles. The shell of a turkey egg takes in oxygen and gives off carbon dioxide. The female turkeys turn the eggs to enable the poults (baby turkeys) to get oxygen. The hens remain on the nests hours a day during incubation.

Then on the twenty-fourth day, the poults begin to make pipping noises in the eggs which are returned by the mother hen, encouraging the babies to burst through the shells. The poults are able to move immediately after birth and quickly adapt to their new environment. The mother leads them away from the egg area, which may attract predators. Biologists have observed new-born poults following their mother all day.

Although somewhat strong at birth and committed to outwitting predators, turkey poults are vulnerable to spring storms and cold and wet weather. They must be kept warm and dry, which is the reason for the high mortality rates of turkeys in springs that have floods and plenty of wet weather.

By the seventh day of life, turkey poults are still adapting to their environment by scratching stones and seeds on the forest floor to feed themselves, and are beginning to fly. By their fourteenth day, the poults are able to fly to their roosts.

In August, turkey poults are two-thirds grown, with males and females still looking alike. But by November or December, the male poults, now known as jakes, which are toms less than one year old, leave their mothers and sisters to form bachelor flocks.

# 2

# Equipment for Turkey Hunting

Turkey hunters of the spring and fall who pit their skills against the bronze baron of the woods must be well equipped. Because the turkey hunter must run, hide, shoot, call and outsmart the bronze baron in the bird's living room, and this wild turkey knows the woods better and can see and hear better than he can, he must have the proper equipment in good working order.

## MEDICINE

Turkey hunters must occasionally sneeze, cough, clear their throats or wipe their runny noses. These seemingly minor noises will spook toms. To suppress these sounds, take a decongestant like Tylenol Sinus before the hunt.

The spring turkey hunter must use a quality insect repellent. You will have a difficult time concentrating on turkeys if mosquitoes or flies buzz in your ears or around your face. More turkeys have been spooked by hunters swatting bugs than for any other reason.

Insect repellent also wards off ticks and red bugs. When you are on a stand waiting for a gobbler to show up and feel a tick crawling up

the back of your neck, you naturally want to squash that tick before the tiny mite can bury its nose deep in your skin. Nevertheless, when a tom in front of you is gobbling, you have to fight the urge to pick the tick.

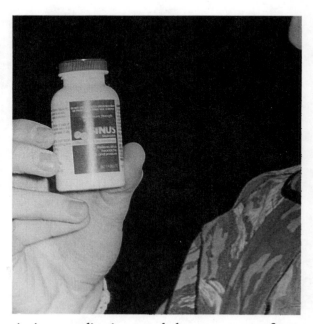

**A sinus medication can help prevent you from clearing your throat, sneezing or coughing while waiting on a turkey stand in the spring woods.**

A quality insect repellent can keep you from swatting mosquitoes and scratching bug bites—movement that will spook a turkey.

I use two types of insect repellent in the turkey woods. An Avon bath oil, Skin So Soft, has a very sweet, feminine smell. Many members of the armed forces apply this product to their skin to protect them from biting insects. I have found that by wiping Skin So Soft all over my body, I rarely if ever get bitten by ticks or red bugs.

To put up a second barrier of defense, I also use a commercially made insect repellent with 25 percent DEET or more. I spray this on my clothing, my boots, the bill of my cap, my headnet and my gloves. But be careful when using this type of repellent; if you fail to let it dry, the repellent may take the finish off your shotgun.

## UNDERCLOTHES

Depending on the weather, I wear either a suit of polypropylene underwear or common cotton underwear. I have discovered that even when hunting in the spring in Texas, long underwear is the preferred underclothing. If you locate a turkey gobbler before daylight, you may have to take a stand and sit still for some time on the cold ground. If you do not dress warmly enough, you will be very uncomfortable and often will begin to shiver and shake before a bird shows up. If you dress too warmly and have to hunt when temperatures are in the 70s and 80s, then you will be miserable the rest of the day. Lightweight underwear with the ability to wick moisture away from the skin will keep you warm in the morning. If temper-

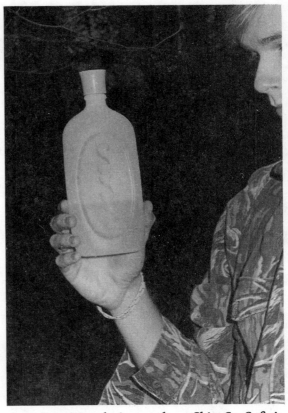

A moisturizing lotion such as Skin So Soft is also an effective insect repellent.

**High-tech underwear wicks moisture away from your skin and keeps you cool and comfortable.**

atures begin to rise during the day, the wicking effect of the underwear actually will cool you down.

In Texas and Mexico, the temperatures in spring may be 40 to 50 degrees in the morning and 80 to 100 degrees later in the day. Long underwear will keep you warm early and cool

later in the day when the temperatures soar.

In the late spring and early fall when the morning temperatures may be in the 50s and 60s, I generally wear cotton briefs and a cotton camo tee-shirt. The camo tee-shirt prevents leaves, sticks, brush and bugs from getting next to my skin.

However, if you wear a white tee-shirt, you are courting danger. White is one of the colors of a turkey's head. If you are sitting next to a tree, that patch of white is at about the same level as a turkey's head. Also you are making the same sounds as a gobbler. If another hunter spots that patch of white and hears the sounds of a wild turkey, you may be in harm's way.

The second reason for not wearing a white tee-shirt is that it may crawl up your neck and become visible when you least expect it. When a gobbler starts coming to your call, he may see that moving patch of white, and be gone.

## BOOTS AND SOCKS

Because the turkey hunter depends so much on his feet, proper footwear is a critical ingredient in successful turkey hunting. Since the sportsman may have to walk, run or wade, he must have footgear that can get him through whatever type of terrain he may encounter in his attempt to get close enough to call a turkey.

Since Cordura cloth uppers on boots can be camouflaged, they allow the hunter to extend his deception all the way to his feet. Boots are available with lightweight Cordura uppers with either rubber, leather or Cordura bottoms, all in camouflage. Make sure the soles of your boots are dark-colored. A turkey may spot light-colored soles.

I also hunt with a two-boot system. My primary pair of boots are lightweight and made of either Gore-Tex and leather or all Gore-Tex. Boots made of this material are usually lighter and more comfortable than either all leather or

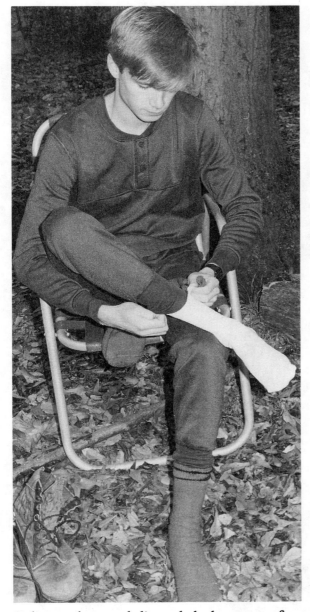

**Polypropylene sock liners help keep your feet dry and comfortable.**

areas I hunt, with the exception of the West, I prefer Vibram to lug soles. Although Vibram soles may have some ripple to them, they are much flatter and lighter than lug soles.

I carry a second pair of boots with me in a daypack, a pair of flyweight stocking-foot waders and a pair of tennis shoes. Although waders may not seem to be turkey hunting equipment, I often locate turkeys on the other side of water that is over boot-top high. But I never let water prevent me from going after my gobbler. If a turkey gobbles on the other side of water, I remove my boots, don my lightweight waders, slip on my tennis shoes and cross the water, coming out dry on the other side.

Under my boots I wear a pair of Thermax or polypropylene socks in either a wool or a cotton blend. My boots fit better with bulky socks, which also provide an added cushion for my feet. Since I have on polypropylene sock liners, my feet remain dry. Today most high-tech socks also have the ability to wick moisture and transfer it to the outside of the sock to keep the foot dry and comfortable.

## CAMOUFLAGE CLOTHING

The camouflage you wear depends on the terrain where you hunt. There are different types of camouflage available to suit a variety of terrain.

### Silhouette Camo

This type of camo is similar to the World War II and Vietnam tiger stripe camo. It consists of large, horizontal bands of foliage colors that break up the outline of the body. The wide bands of color help the hunter to blend into the shadows and foliage of his environment.

rubber boots. I also choose boots that support my ankles and are waterproof.

Selecting the proper sole for turkey hunting is important too. Lug soles pick up mud, dirt and clay, and add weight to your feet. In the spring, flooded areas and mud are commonplace across much of the United States. In most

Lightweight waterproof boots help you move through the woods silently and comfortably. Camo uppers are an added feature that aids concealment.

When I have to cross a stream or swamp, I don my chest-high waders and put my camo boots in my backpack.

## Vertical Patterns

Vertical-pattern camos are based on the theory that most of the colors in the woods are vertical like tree trunks. This camo is composed of large oblongs about two to three inches long consisting of different shades of gray, black and brown that attempt to match the colors of many hardwood trees. This pattern has replaced many of the WWII patterns and gained acceptance among turkey hunters, who usually sit next to trees. A turkey hunter should wear the vertical pattern that most resembles the tree trunks in the forest he hunts.

Another vertical pattern has smaller blocks of color in tones of brown instead of brown and gray. This pattern has sold well and has created a stir in the camo market. I have worn it in the swamps of Florida and the deserts of New Mexico and have found it to be a universal pattern that fits most terrain.

Two other vertical patterns consist primarily of browns and blacks to match darker woods and earth tones, and a bluish camo with smaller bars to match pine trees.

## Blend-In Camo

If you ever see a hen mallard duck, notice that her coloring blends in with the bulrushes and weeds along the edge of the water. Mother Nature has devised a color scheme that matches the feathers of the hen to her surroundings. Blend-in camo tries to do the same. Blend-in patterns often simulate leaves and bushes. A new type of blend-in camo is designed for hunters who use treestands and suggests tree limbs crossing vertical patchwork.

## All-Purpose Camo

All-purpose camo is predominantly brown and combines all three camouflage patterns. Although the pattern basically is vertical, it also has leaves and branches on it. The placement

**Brigade Quartermaster's ASAT pattern, modeled after WWII camo suits, breaks up your silhouette and works in most terrain.**

and the colors of the leaves and the branches break up the silhouette of the hunter so he blends in with his surroundings.

All these camouflage patterns hide the hunter from the turkey. Discuss camo with other turkey hunters in your area and your local sporting goods dealers to determine which kind is the most appropriate for the region you hunt and the season. Here are a few guidelines:

In early spring before the leaves are thick, I usually choose a vertical, all-bark pattern. At this time, the turkey sees mainly tree trunks since few leaves are on the trees. During the middle of the spring, as the leaves begin to appear and more shadows are present in the woods, I often select a leaf pattern type of camo at least for the shirt and either a bark pattern or a silhouette-breaking pattern for the pants. I try to match the ground cover with my pants and the foliage cover with my shirt.

In the late spring, most of the trees have their leaves. For that reason I generally pick a green leaf-pattern camo or a silhouette-breaking camo because there is so much shadow and shade in the woods.

## Pants and Shirts

Features to look for in pants for turkey hunting are drawstrings at the bottom and double-knee protection. They should be somewhat longer than your regular pants. The drawstrings will keep your cuffs from catching on bushes and brush, they will help to hide your socks, which may ride above the tops of your boots, and they

## POPULAR CAMO PATTERNS

Hide 'N Pine pattern in bluish tones and small bars simulates a background of conifers.

Realtree's vertical pattern helps the hunter blend in with all types of trees in the forest.

will keep sticks and bugs from coming up your pant legs.

I like double-knee pants. An aggressive turkey hunter does a considerable amount of crawling and needs that extra layer of material over the knees. Double bottoms also keep the seat of the pants from wearing out.

If your pants are somewhat longer than usual, they won't ride up when you're seated and expose your leg—which could possibly spook a turkey.

I like chamois-type pants better than pants of cotton. They are softer, quieter, and more comfortable than other hunting pants. I prefer a six-pocketed pant because I always have plenty of turkey hunting gear to go in those pockets. The pants should have buttons and not velcro or zippers. Buttons are quieter than velcro or zippers.

Mossy Oak's Full Foliage combines vertical, horizontal, and leaf patterns in one suit.

Trebark was one of the first vertical patterns in camouflage clothing.

The pants also need large belt loops and buttons inside them for suspenders. I have found that suspenders are more comfortable and prevent binding at the waist when you sit down.

A camo shirt should have an extra-long tail so that it doesn't ride up and expose your back. Select a shirt that is a size larger than normal; having excess material at your wrist will ensure that you won't show skin when you bring your gun up and possibly spook a turkey.

### Headnets, Gloves and Hats

No camo or hunting aid will prevent a turkey from seeing you if you do not sit still. Generally a turkey spots the hunter not because he is wearing improper camo but because he moves.

There are as many styles of headnets and gloves as camouflage manufacturers, and each turkey hunter can tell you why he prefers the style he chooses. I like a soft cotton glove with an extra-long wristband that comes five or six inches up the arm to cover any gap that may appear below my shirt sleeve. A soft cotton glove not only protects my hand from insects, briars and sticks but also allows me to feel my trigger and safety. Generally I match my gloves with the same camo pattern I am wearing on my shirt.

I prefer a full-face headnet usually made out of cloth rather than netting material, although netting material lets you hear better. A cloth headnet totally hides the head and neck and prevents these areas from being attacked by bugs, which is a concern of mine when I hunt in the South in the springtime. I favor an elastic or a drawstring system in the headnet. Then I can secure it, and the opening for the eyes will not move around. Since I wear glasses, often I wear one of the wire-frame types of headnets.

I like a camouflage hat with an adjustable headband and prefer a baseball-cap style. A hat is a very important piece of the total camo suit. When properly worn, the hat helps hide you, and the bill of the cap keeps the sun out of your eyes and helps to hide the whites of your eyeballs from a turkey when you are low on the stock of your gun and aiming down the barrel.

### Turkey Vest

Another essential piece of equipment for the turkey hunter is a vest with a large back game pocket that is big enough to carry a turkey. A turkey vest has external pockets where you can carry calls, shells, extra gloves and other equipment you will need. I like a vest that also has internal pockets with zippers or some type of closure other than velcro, which is noisy. These pockets can store binoculars, lunches and other equipment.

A quality turkey vest also should have a camouflaged drop seat that is long enough and wide enough to allow you to lower the seat and sit comfortably on the ground. Some turkey vests feature a cushion in the back, which adds comfort. Often turkey vests come equipped with a blaze orange flag that can be let down over the back of the game bag when a successful hunter comes out of the woods with his bird.

A turkey vest with adjustable straps and some type of fastening in the front allows you to sprint through the woods without your equipment bouncing out the front of your vest as you get into position to call a turkey. A vest's pockets must be big enough to hold box calls and friction calls as well as diaphragm calls.

In my turkey vest, I always carry a camouflage rainsuit. If you hunt throughout the spring, you will doubtless get caught in a shower.

## BLINDS

Blinds serve several functions and can be constructed in various ways. Portable blinds, which let you move behind the blind even as the

Camo turkey vest has external pockets for calls, shells and other equipment for a turkey hunt with room to pack your bird out of the woods.

Blaze orange flag attached to the back of a hunting vest can help prevent accidents.

Camouflage rainsuit fits easily into your vest and allows you to hunt during spring rains.

turkey approaches, are particularly effective if you are using a box call, a pushbutton call or a friction call and must move your hands when calling. Blinds are also very helpful for hunters who have trouble sitting still long enough to call a turkey. Many bowhunters have found blinds make bagging a gobbler with a bow much easier. Because a bowhunter must draw to shoot, a turkey often will spot the archer before he can launch an arrow. A blind that totally covers the hunter yet provides shooting ports can give him a decided advantage.

When selecting a blind, choose one that is lightweight, easy to carry and sets up quickly. The stakes should be of strong, lightweight metal and go into the ground easily.

You may choose to use a natural blind if you are an experienced hunter. Carry pruning shears and you easily can cut small limbs and bushes to set up in front of a tree where you plan to take a stand. When possible, I make some type of natural blind to break up my outline and allow me to move if necessary when a turkey approaches. Three or four small limbs and bushes will do the job. You can also use pruning shears to trim limbs and bushes in your line of fire.

## BINOCULARS

Binoculars allow you not only to see the bird at great distances but more importantly to determine its sex. I use two different types of binoculars.

I like small, compact binoculars that I can wear around my neck and put in my vest. With them I can quickly determine the sex of a turkey. I can also read the mood of the gobbler before he comes in, which helps me to determine the types of calls to use. I also use a bigger, heavier set of binoculars for field checking. I carry them at midday when I'm scouting for turkeys by car and in the evening in the woods when I try to spot turkeys flying up to their roost. Larger binoculars are brighter and let me distinguish gobblers from hens. Then I know where to set up the next morning.

## RANGEFINDERS

A rangefinder accurately determines your distance from the bird. Then you know when you squeeze the trigger that the pattern you have shot on the shooting range will cover the turkey's head and neck.

Redfield's waterproof binoculars have an instant-focusing device that provides a sharp image beyond 30 feet without manual adjustment. Nitrogen-filled barrels prevent leaking or fogging. Soft rubber eye cups fold back for eyeglass wearers.

Nikon Mountaineer 8 × 23 Binoculars are waterproof and fogproof, weigh only 15 ounces. Diopter adjustment permits regulating lenses for individual eye strength.

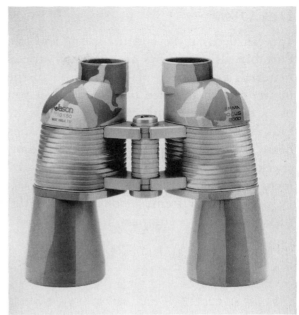

Jason's Perma Focus 2000 Camouflage Binoculars come in 7 × 21 and 7 × 35. Both have wide fields of view—the 7 × 21, 393 feet; the 7 × 35, 578 feet. Weights are 7 and 23.7 ounces respectively.

Pentax 7 × 20 and 9 × 20 DCF roof-prism, center-focusing binoculars are compact and lightweight (7.4 ounces). Housing is rubber-coated to provide protection against moisture, shock and corrosion.

Zeiss Pocket Binoculars are available in 6 × 20, 8 × 20 and 10 × 25. B-type eyepieces allow full-field viewing for wearers of prescription glasses. Hinged barrels fold into a compact unit that fits in shirt pocket.

## DECOYS

You can decoy turkeys in the spring and fall. Portable turkey decoys are made of various materials and can be placed in front of the hunter to imitate a hen or a jake. When you use a decoy along with calling, you give the tom the opportunity to see what he thinks he's heard. Before you hunt with a turkey decoy, check with your local fish and game department since decoys are not legal in all states.

Several other items I consider essential turkey gear are a compass, a flashlight and candy bars.

Turkey hunting is an exciting sport and can be very enjoyable for the hunter who has the proper equipment. Guns, shells and scopes will be discussed later; these basic essentials are what you need to begin the sport of turkey hunting. Comfort, fit and function are the three key words to consider when choosing equipment. The more comfortable you are in the woods, the longer you can sit still, the easier you can move through the woods, and the more enjoyable will be your hunt for a wily gobbler.

# 3

# Guns, Shells and Accessories

In the days of the mountain men, a turkey shoot was an event. Men with flintlocks or percussion-cap rifles attempted to shoot a live, tied-at-the-foot turkey in the head as the bird ducked and dodged behind some type of cover. You had to be a dead shot to hit a turkey under those conditions. Today, with binoculars and shotguns, taking a turkey is not that difficult. However, as most turkey hunting experts say, "If you hunt turkeys long enough, you will miss some."

What causes us to miss turkeys? Can we reduce the number of misses? One way is to choose the right gun and use hunting aids and new sighting devices.

No matter which gun you shoot, if you cannot judge accurately the range of a bird, you will not be able to determine the effectiveness of your shot. Even if you know the effective range of the gun, you will be unsure whether the pattern will put enough pellets in the gobbler to bring him down. Misjudging distance is easy. If you are a new hunter, you will be unaccustomed to seeing a turkey in the woods. When a turkey

stands erect, he may look much bigger than you expect. Judging distance is the first step in understanding the patterning of your gun.

When you are in the woods, try to judge a certain distance from your stand, say 10 yards. That will help you to estimate 20, 30 yards, etc. Pick out a landmark at each distance as a reference point. Then when a turkey appears, you will know whether or not he is within range.

One of the best techniques for determining distance is to use a rangefinder. Often when a hunter uses a rangefinder, he believes he is doing so to determine the distance to the bird. He brings the rangefinder to his eye, focuses it on the target, reads the distance, puts it back in his pocket, picks up his gun and prepares for the shot. But this much movement spooks the turkey and is not the most effective way to use a rangefinder.

A better way to use a rangefinder is before you sight a turkey. Guess the distances of landmarks in the woods, and then use the rangefinder to check your estimates. This way, you will train your eyes. The more you prac-

**A turkey shoot was a major event for the early mountain men.**

tice, the better you will be at judging distances, and the more prepared you will be when a turkey appears.

Another method of using a rangefinder is to check the distance from your calling position to different landmarks in your field of view. Then wait until a gobbler walks into the effective area, usually within 35 yards.

Most importantly, never force a shot. Do not shoot unless the turkey is in range. This requires mental and physical discipline. But by exercising self-restraint, and then moving to a new position and calling again, you will increase your chances of actually bagging the bird.

Many turkey hunters spend hours practicing their calling but very little time practicing judging distances. If a hunter calls a turkey in but does not know its range when he shoots, chances are he will miss the bird. Before you pattern your shotgun or decide on which shells

to use, practice being the best judge of distance you can be.

Many hunters believe the phrase "patterning a shotgun" means standing 30 yards from a target, squeezing the trigger and determining how many pellets have put tiny holes in the paper. If this is your method, you may be missing more turkeys than you are bagging. One shot does not yield enough information.

To pattern your shotgun, put targets at 10, 20, 30, 40 and 50 yards. Then you can see what your gun will do at several different ranges. If you miss your shot when a turkey is at close range, it's probably because the pattern is too tight. If the turkey is farther away, the pattern opens up and the pellets are distributed over a larger area.

When patterning your shotgun, try to shoot at the targets from the same position you expect to be shooting at a gobbler in the woods. For most, this means sitting with your back against a tree.

## SHOTSHELLS

Every hunter has his own opinion of the best shot size for turkey hunting. The gun, not the hunter, should dictate what size shot is used.

Your shotgun will pattern every shot size differently. A shotgun that may throw No. 6 shot all over the paper and only place one or two pellets in the kill zone may hold a tight pattern with No. 4s, putting six to ten pellets in the kill zone. Some shotguns hold a tight, close pattern when shooting duplex shells, and some do not. Duplex shells are a combination of No. 2s and No. 4s, while others combine No. 4s and No. 6s. The best way to learn which is best in your gun is to shoot a variety of shot at various distances, no matter what works best for your hunting buddy.

Another factor that plays a major role in the effectiveness of a shell is the brand name. Remember, various brands pattern differently in the same gun. The best way to determine which shell and shot produces the best pattern in your gun is to buy several brands in the same shot size and test each at varying distances. If you do not like what you see, move on to another shot size, and repeat the test.

### When Is the Shell at Fault?

The big Merriam turkey I had seen coming from 50 yards away was in full strut reflecting all the hues of his feathers. The bird's head seemed to glow. His white crown, his red wattles and the blue around his eyes and throat lit up like neon lights against the dark background of green, black and bronze.

When I clucked, the tom dropped his strut and raised his noble head. I squeezed the trigger and was ready to make the 20-yard trot to recover the flopping bird. But this turkey did not flop. Instantly he changed from a proud tom to a nervous one and took off. I was dumbfounded. And of course I blamed the shotshell. Shotshells are to the turkey hunter what fishing line is to the bass angler. If the shells fail or do not produce as they have been designed to, then the hunter misses, and the turkey escapes. The shells you shoot will determine the turkeys you take.

According to Dick Dietz, public relations manager for Remington Arms Company, "Because turkey hunters generally do not shoot large numbers of shells, I advise them to pay a little more money and buy the best shells they can get. If they plan to shoot cases of shells like dove hunters do, then price is a consideration. However, most turkey hunters rarely will shoot more than five to ten shotshells per season. If the best shells cost a nickel or a dime more, the wisest thing they can do is pay the extra money to ensure a successful hunt."

The best shells shoot pellets that fly straight. As Dietz explains, "To shoot a tight pattern, the shot needs to stay as perfectly round as possible. If the shot becomes bent or uneven, it will have an uneven surface and fly erratically."

What causes shot to fly straight? Dietz says several factors are involved, including buffering, the amount of antimony in the shot, and the shot cup itself.

"Buffering is a polyethylene material that is put into the shotshell with the shot and fills in the spaces between the pellets. The proper buffering is more important as the pellet size gets bigger. The initial impact of the firing can cause the pellets to be scrunched down and deformed. Buffering reduces shot deformity. I suggest a turkey hunter consider a buffered shell if he's using a larger shot such as No. 4.

"The amount of antimony in shot determines its hardness. A harder shot seems to deform less and fly straighter. However, you can't add more than a certain amount of antimony to it without losing the weight and density that give the shot good ballistics. A high antimony shot is about 6 percent antimony and makes for a good turkey shot.

"Also, the shot cup inside the shell is critical to the shell's performance. This plastic cup acts as an overpowder ceiling wad and seals the powder's gases behind the shot column. Too, the shot cup encases the pellets and keeps them from getting deformed by touching the inside of the barrel. The cushioning at the bottom of the shot cup reduces the impact of the shot when the shell is fired and thereby reduces pellet deformation."

I prefer a copper-plated shot, because I believe copper plating tends to make the pellets harder and thus they fly straighter. But Dietz chuckles and says that, "Copper plating does make the shot look prettier besides making the outer surface of the pellets a little harder and reducing deformation. But, since the copper is a very, very thin coating around the lead, we really don't know how much harder the copper-coated shells are."

When I load my gun to go turkey hunting, I usually place No. 6 shot in the barrel of my automatic and have two No. 4s behind it. My thinking is that I want the densest shot pattern possible at close range. Then if I miss, the heavier No. 4 shot can inflict more damage even with fewer pellets at a greater distance.

Some of my hunting buddies have just the opposite philosophy. They choose the heavier No. 4s as their first shots, believing they have more knock-down power, and use the smaller No. 6s as back-ups for taking a second shot at a running turkey.

When I asked Dietz what shot size was best for the turkey hunter, he told me about a survey he had conducted.

"I asked thirty of the nation's best turkey hunters and guides what shot size they preferred," Dietz recalls. "At that time, No. 6s were favored by the majority of top flight turkey hunters with No. 4s coming in second. They told me they wanted pellets that were hard enough and big enough to get penetration into the turkey's head, yet they wanted enough pellets to produce a very dense pattern. They seemed to think No. 6s gave the best combination of pellet size and pellet density."

A few years ago Remington introduced a duplex shell which combined two different shot sizes in the same shell. The idea was to make the ultimate turkey load and to solve the age-old problem of which should the hunter shoot, No. 4s or No. 6s? With the duplex load, the hunter could shoot both shots in the same shell.

"The duplex shells were an attempt to provide a range of pellet size at a given distance from the bird you'd be shooting," Dietz explained. "In the beginning, our company had hoped to come up with an alternative shell. The duplex shells on the average patterned better than the single pellet loads since the hunter got a denser and a more evenly distributed pattern with the duplex shells.

"I recommend the $4 \times 6$ duplex shell for turkey hunting. This shell gives the turkey hunter the 6 shot he seems to prefer, but also has some 4s in the pattern to produce better penetration than the 6s alone will provide. The 4s also will add a little more penetration when a hunter is taking a shot at a turkey on the outer fringes of acceptable turkey shooting range. These duplex shells pattern so well that usually you will have about as many shots in the killing diameter of the pattern as you do with No. 5s."

The best way to know whether you prefer duplex or single-shot shells is to take both types to a patterning board and test them yourself.

When the 3-inch magnum shotguns first came on the market, turkey hunters adopted this bigger shotgun like a brother and assumed it would increase the range at which they could take a turkey. Some hunters even moved up to a 10-gauge gun and shell so that they would be able to reach out and touch a turkey at greater distances.

Although I always had believed the bigger shells would cause pellets to shoot further, Dietz mentions that, "In terms of pellet energy, you don't get any more range with a 2¾-inch shell than you do with a 10-gauge shell. Pellet energy is determined by the size of the pellet and the speed at which it starts. Even though you move up in size of shotshell, you don't really get any more range.

"However, at any range, when you go up in shell casing size, you add more capacity for the shot, which means you add more shot. For instance, more shot is present in a 3-inch shell than in a 2¾-inch shell. As you go up in shotshell size and increase the number of pellets the shell will hold, you can produce a denser pattern at a greater distance. A 10-gauge shell will hold more pellets than either a 3-inch shell or a 2¾-inch shell. Therefore, the larger shell will produce a denser pattern even at a greater range."

Just as the bass fisherman has learned all he can about better lines to catch and hold more and bigger fish, turkey hunters need to understand more about the shells we shoot and how to select the best ones.

## CHOOSING A TURKEY GUN

The shotgun you choose to hunt gobblers should be as personal as your signature, fit you as comfortably as a new suit of underwear, and be as dependable as a good friend.

Allen Jenkins of Liberty, Mississippi, president of M.L. Lynch Calls, uses a distinctive turkey hunting strategy that suits him. No one could mistake Jenkins for an offensive end for the Chicago Bears; rather, he resembles a bantamweight boxer. The gun Jenkins prefers is a double-barreled, 20-gauge Browning Citori with modified and full barrels, which seems more appropriate for quail than turkey—unless you know Jenkins, who is a master turkey caller.

"For me, the sport of turkey hunting is to be able to master the bird with my knowledge and calling skills," Jenkins says. "To take a shot, I first have to outsmart the turkey. If I can call a gobbler in to less than 30 yards of where I'm sitting, then I've defeated the bird and have the right to decide whether I want to take him or let him go. If I can't get the bird closer than 30 yards, he wins the game, outsmarts me and leaves with his life.

"I'm not saying this is how every turkey hunter should hunt, but it is my style. If I'll be taking shots at less than 30 yards, then why would I carry a cannon into the woods? The Browning Citori is lightweight, comfortable to carry, tightly patterns No. 4 shot and tumbles the toms I defeat. In other words, that gun does all I ask it to do."

Allen Jenkins' shotgun is his trademark. If calling a gobbler in close is more important to you than actually bagging a bird, then a small-gauge gun is appropriate. However, others who want more range opt for larger-gauge guns.

Eddie Salter of Brewton, Alabama, has won the World Turkey Calling Contest twice and has been hunting turkeys all of his life in the heart of some of the best turkey habitat in the nation. Salter, who is built like a middle linebacker, reads a situation and then sets his course to seek and destroy. The gun Salter chooses must be accurate and powerful. Salter is also a traditionalist who believes that if his shotgun has proven deadly accurate under all hunting situations, then why should he change?

"The longer the sighting plane you have, the more accurately you will be able to sight and shoot turkeys," Salter explains. "That's why I shoot a Remington 1100 12 gauge with a 30-inch barrel. I've always used a long-barreled gun and have bagged my fair share of turkeys with this longer barrel. I really don't hunt in cover that thick. The ability to move the gun to shoot between trees is not that big a problem for me. I'm accustomed to the weight of the gun and don't consider it a handicap. I'm willing to walk or run a long way to a turkey. I use all my knowledge and skill to get that bird into a place where I can take him. To compromise two or three inches on the length of the barrel or an ounce or two in the weight of the gun and give up the accuracy of the longer sighting plane just doesn't seem to make much sense to me."

The ethics of hunting wild turkeys vary according to region. Your pleasure may be another's sin. In many areas of the West, bagging a longbeard with a rifle, which many easterners consider a mortal sin, is as acceptable as cheering for your team at a football game. Many who hunt the West with rifles will take a longbeard with whatever rifle they happen to have handy at the time. However, most prefer the .222 or the .243 for hunting turkeys.

When you start hunting turkeys, your primary concern as a beginner is to bag a gobbler—whether it is a longbeard, has a short beard or almost no beard at all. Next you usually look for only longbeard gobblers because they're more of a challenge. Then as you mature and have the opportunity to bag more turkeys, you may concentrate on spur length. For instance, Allen Jenkins constantly looks at a gobbler's foot as the bird comes in to where he is calling. If the turkey does not have spurs longer than one inch, Jenkins will not shoot.

The final step of maturity for a turkey hunter is to search for a more challenging way to bag a tom. You may decide to try to take a turkey with a bow or a muzzleloader. In my first muzzleloading season, I shot a Connecticut Valley Arms turkey special, which is a single-shot, blackpowder 12 gauge with screw-in chokes.

Blackpowder shotguns do not pattern like conventional shotguns do. They require more time on the pattern board, more patience and much more shooting than conventional guns to be able to understand what will happen to your shot pattern when you squeeze the trigger. I have discovered that to put enough shot consistently into a turkey head silhouette with my blackpowder gun, the target has to be at less than twenty steps, which means I will have a very challenging hunt.

## POPULAR TURKEY GUNS

At this writing, the following guns are available for the turkey hunter. Once you decide which style of hunting you prefer, you can pick the gun that suits you best.

### Winchester Turkey Gun

The National Wild Turkey Federation has selected the Winchester Model 1300 12-gauge turkey gun made by U.S. Repeating Arms Co., Inc., as gun of the year. This gun weighs only 7 pounds and features a checkered, camouflaged stock and forearm, a nonreflective matte finish

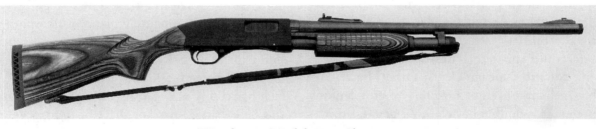

**Winchester Model 1300 Shotgun.**

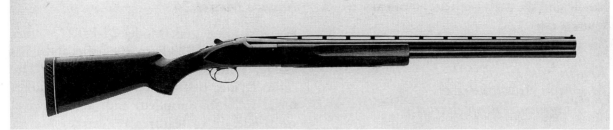

**Double barreled, 20-gauge Browning Citori.**

**BPS Game Gun with 20½-inch barrels.**

and an engraved receiver. A pump action, the gun operates with Winchester's Armor-Lock Rotary Belt system. It comes with a sling, swivels and a recoil pad. The 22-inch barrel is equipped with Winchester's floating vent rib and Winchoke tubes in extra full, full and modified.

## Citori Lightning and BPS Pump

Browning's Citori Lightning 3½-inch 12-gauge over-and-under and BPS 3½-inch 12-gauge pump are versatile shotguns chambered in the newest 12-gauge cartridge. Their back-bored barrels (.754 bore) come with Browning's new Invector Plus threaded choke tubes that are designed to handle the extra demands of 3½-inch magnum loads.

The Citori Lightning 3½-inch magnum 12 gauge will be available with 30-inch or 28-inch barrels in Grade I only. The stock and forearm are of select walnut with a highgloss finish, a classic rounded pistol grip and a trim forearm.

The average weight of the 30-inch model is 8 pounds, 9 ounces, and the 28-inch model weighs 8 pounds, 5 ounces.

The Browning BPS Pump 3½-inch magnum 12 gauge, weighing in at 8 pounds, 12 ounces, is offered in standard Hunting or Stalker models with 30-inch or 28-inch barrel, and features a new graphite-fiberglass composite stock.

## Remington SP-10 Magnum

In designing the new SP-10 Magnum, a 10-gauge autoloading shotgun, Remington has included a new trigger group, and a gas system with two vents to reduce powder residue build-up on critical moving surfaces. Further improvements in the shotgun's overall design include a new feeding and extraction system and the addition of an elastomer buffer to the slide extension for shock resistance. All critical cam, pivot and retaining pins have been designed for maximum strength and durability. Gas system components, bolt, carrier, operating handle and shellstop latch are all constructed of stainless steel.

### Remington 11-87 SP Magnum Autoloader & SP Magnum Pump Action

These two guns work exceptionally well with regular full Rem Chokes. However, they provide even denser, tighter patterns with the new Remington Extra Full optional turkey chokes that produce 80 percent plus patterns with most popular turkey loads —No. 4s, 6s and Duplex 4 × 6s. Their relatively short 26-inch barrels, dull wood and metal finishes, carrying slings and 3-inch chambers make them ideal for turkey hunting.

This pump-action gun with 3-inch chambers, interchangeable Rem Choke system, straight English stock and 21-inch barrel is a handy gun to carry into the woods for gobblers.

### Savage Model 24

Savage's turkey gun, Model 24-F-12T, comes with a .222 or a .223 Rem rifle barrel and a 12-gauge, 3-inch magnum bottom tube. The camo Rynite stock, interchangeable chokes (extra-full tube supplied) and factory swivel studs add up to features any turkey hunter appreciates.

### Mossberg Model 500 Camo

When sportsmen expressed a need for a camo shotgun, Mossberg responded with the 12-gauge Model 500 Camo that is designed specifically to the requirements of turkey hunters. It features a drilled and tapped receiver for scope bases, quick detachable swivels, camo sling and a tough, synthetic stock and forearm. The Speedfeed models give you quick access to as many as four extra rounds spring-loaded in the buttstock.

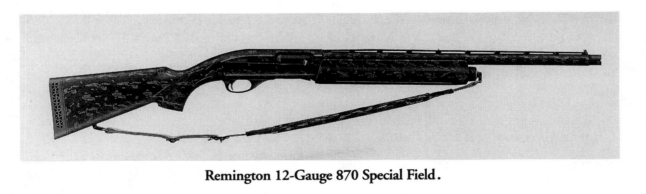

**Remington 12-Gauge 870 Special Field.**

**Savage Model 24-F-12T.**

**Weatherby Orion Grade I Shotgun.**

## Mossberg Model 500 Turkey/Deer Camo Combo

This 12-gauge pump gun combo comes with two interchangeable barrels, a 20-inch Accu-Choke and a 24-inch slugster. It has a synthetic forearm and a Speedfeed buttstock, is drilled and tapped for scope mounting, and includes swivels and a camo web sling.

## Classic Model 101 Waterfowler

This over-and-under shotgun, originally made for Winchester, now is offered exclusively by Classic Doubles. With a 30-inch barrel, nonglare finish on buttstock and forearm along with a matte finish on both barrel and frame, the Waterfowler is the perfect shotgun for ducks and geese as well as turkey when extra concealment is mandatory. The stock and forearm are made of the highest grade semi-fancy American walnut.

## Parker Hale Model 645E-XXV S × S

A 16-gauge field gun manufactured in Spain by Ignacio Ugartechea, S.A., to the specification of Parker Hale, Ltd., of Birmingham, England, and imported into the U.S. by Precision Sports, the Model 645-E-XXV is an ideal upland gun. Weighing 6 pounds, 6 ounces and measuring only 42³⁄₁₆ inches overall, it is a typical Churchill variety, except for being 16 gauge. The barrels actually measure 25³⁄₁₆ inches long, complete with tapered center rib. This gun handles well and produces excellent patterns.

## Weatherby Over-And-Under Shotguns

Weatherby has added three new grades to their existing line of over-and-under shotguns. The Athena Grade V has a much more detailed, intricate engraving pattern than the existing model which has been renamed the Athena Grade IV. The same attention to detail is applied from the precision mating of barrels to the hand checkered stock.

Two new grades have been added to the existing Orion. The Orion Grade III has game-bird scenes engraved on a silver-gray nitride-finished receiver, which complements the beautiful Claro walnut stock. The existing Orion shotgun is now identified as the Grade II. Added to this series is the Orion Grade I, which has a richly blued receiver with no engraving and a lesser grade of stock wood. The buttstock is fitted with a plastic buttplate rather than a recoil pad. The Athena and the Orion come in 12-gauge field models.

## Stoeger IGA Single-Barrel Shotgun

This rugged top-break shotgun features a

Stoeger/IGA Reuna-Single Barrel with choke tube.

Stoeger/IGA Uplander-Side by Side with choke tubes.

Benelli Montefeltro Super 90 Uplander.

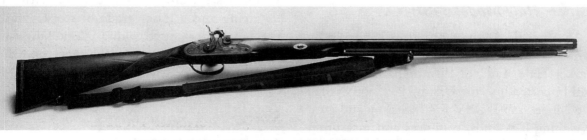

Connecticut Valley Arms PS219 Trapper Shotgun.

unique locking system. Pulling rearward on the trigger guard releases the underlug engagement, thus opening the action. Simple mechanical extraction allows for convenient removal of spent shells. A half-cocked setting on the hammer provides the safety mode. The stock and semi-beavertail forend are of durable Brazilian hardwood.

### Stoeger IGA Side-By-Side Uplander Shotgun

This gun will provide years of trouble-free, dependable performance. A vice-tight, super-safe locking system is provided by two massive underlugs. The safety is automatic. The solid sighting rib is matte finished for glare-free sighting. Barrels are of Moly-Chrome steel with micropolished bores to give dense, consistent patterns and are formulated specifically for use with steel shot. The stock and forend are hand-checkered in durable hardwood.

### Benelli Montefeltro Super-90 Turkey Shotgun

This 7-pound, 1-ounce 12 gauge with 3-inch chamber has an inertia recoil, and the Montefeltro rotating bolt-operating system with a five magazine capacity. The barrel length is 24 inches; the gun's overall length, 43 inches. The screw-in chokes for this satin walnut stocked gun with matte-black finish include full, improved and modified. It is imported by Heckler & Koch, Inc.

### CVA Trapper Shotgun

This 5½-pound, 46-inch long 12-gauge muzzleloader comes with three easy to change interchangeable chokes: improved, modified and full. The single barrel is mounted on a select hardwood stock, which features an English-style straight grip, and is fired by an authentic

v-type mainspring lock. Overall length is 46 inches. The 28-inch barrel has a brass bead front sight, hooked breech and a snail-type bolster with convenient cleanout screw.

### Nu-Line 2.5-Inch Turkey Hunter Tubes

These tubes have been produced for turkey hunting with No. 2, 4 or 6 lead shot. The tubes have an extra-long conical lead and a specifically designed choke for tighter, denser patterns, resulting in clean, one-shot kills.

## SCOPES

A turkey hunter can improve his marksmanship skills and his chances of making a successful shot by adding a high-quality scope to his shotgun. Some of the better scopes for turkey hunting are shown below.

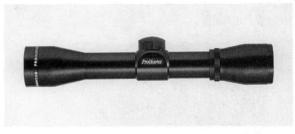

**Simmons shotgun scopes are parallax-free at fifty yards for accuracy at short range.**

**Top, the ProHunter 4 × 32mm scope; below, the Deeerfield 2.5 × 20mm.**

Redfield 1×–4× variable scope is tooled from a single tube; hand-fitted lenses shrug off magnum recoils with ease.

Zeiss Diavari-C 1.5–4.5× 18T riflescope is lightweight and low-mounting—ideal for mounting on a shotgun.

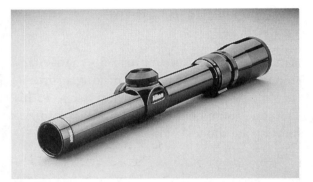

Nikon 1.5–4.5× 30 variable scope is a good balance between magnification and field of view for turkey hunting.

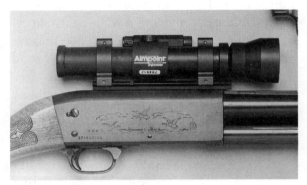

Aimpoint 2-Power scope has a fixed, low-power electronic sight with a floating red dot and built in magnification.

# 4

# Scouting for Turkeys

The hunters who successfully bag their birds each season are the ones who spend more time scouting and less time hunting. Generally turkeys stay in the same area, rarely wandering more than a mile and a half from where they roost. If you can pinpoint where turkeys are roosting or feeding, or strutting, dusting, bugging or loafing, you usually can find them in the same places at the same time every day. But to locate specific turkeys, you first must find land on which to hunt.

## PUBLIC LANDS

Many states have national forests, which have been set aside by the federal government to ensure wild places for Americans to hunt, fish, camp, hike and enjoy the outdoors. Often national forest lands have huntable populations of wild turkeys.

Begin your search for wild turkeys by calling the U.S. Forest Service, which should be listed in your phone book. If you cannot find the number of the U.S. Forest Service, call your state's Department of Conservation or your local game warden/conservation officer and ask for the phone number. Then contact the U.S. Forest Service, and ask them which area of the national forest in your section of the country should provide the best turkey hunting. Get the phone number of the area ranger, and call him to set up an appointment. Ask him to bring a map of the close-by national forests that have turkeys.

When you meet with the ranger, study the map. Have him recommend where to hunt for turkeys. The forest ranger should know more about the national forest than anyone else since usually he is in the forest daily.

Your next choice will be state game lands, often called wildlife management areas. Most states usually have an area manager for each of their game lands who patrols the areas daily and will be able to tell you where and how to hunt turkeys. Ask the area manager to mark a map of the region to pinpoint where you most likely will discover turkeys.

Next talk to large landowners in your state—timber companies, utility companies, coal com-

# WHERE TO FIND TURKEYS

When you are scouting for turkeys, try to find their roost tree, their feeding, strutting and dusting grounds. They usually return to the same places every day.

**ROOST TREE**

**FEEDING GROUNDS**

**STRUTTING GROUNDS**

**DUSTING GROUNDS**

panies and large corporations which own vast tracts of woodlands. By contacting these corporations and determining if they have lands for the public to hunt either through a fee or a paid permit system, you often will locate good turkey hunting lands close to your home.

Another quick yet reliable way to find both public and private lands for hunting turkeys is to contact the conservation officer or game warden in the area you want to hunt, because these men usually patrol one to three counties per day. They know which companies own the best turkey land, and whether or not the land is open to public or private hunting. Because they are defenders of wildlife, they will also know the hunting policies of the landowners whose property they patrol.

## PRIVATE LANDS

When I started college in Livingston, Alabama, which was situated in a very rural county, I did not know anyone in the area. There was an abundance of woodlots, with probably more turkeys than almost anyplace in the world. So I began my research at the center of all information in any community, the barber shop. The barber will probably know the men who own turkey hunting land and can direct you to them. Also, the priest or the pastor of the largest church in a community will be aware of which of his parishoners hunt turkeys and/or own turkey lands. Another source for locating turkey hunting lands is the banker. Landowners often must borrow money, and they need the services of a banker. Most bankers I have met in rural communities hunt or know who owns huntable land. Also contact the county sheriff. The sheriff's department compiles information on everyone in the county. He will know who owns property and your chances for obtaining permission to hunt there. He even may help you to get permission. Finally, con-

The rural letter carrier can help you find lands on which to hunt turkeys.

sult the rural letter carrier, who knows everybody in an area.

## LOCATING TURKEYS

Once you have found a place to hunt, you have to locate the turkeys. The simplest method is to ask the landowner. If you are hunting public lands, ask the forest ranger, wildlife management area director or game warden. All of them will know the general areas where turkeys roost. But you still have to pinpoint their location.

The best way to do this is to go into the woods before daylight and listen for gobbling. Novice turkey hunters often take turkey calls

When you move into the woods to locate gobblers before the season, carry only crow, owl or hawk calls, but not turkey calls.

with them and call when a turkey gobbles. This is a mistake. Instead, I recommend that you leave your calls at home when you scout for birds. When you are scouting, you just want to pinpoint the location of the turkeys. The more you call a turkey, the more accustomed he'll become to calling and the more wary he'll be when the season opens. When you go into the woods before the season, carry only a crow call, an owl call or a hawk call. These calls will make a turkey gobble but won't bring him to you.

## Mark Maps

When scouting before the season, take a topographical map and an aerial photo of the land you plan to hunt with you. In most regions, a topographical map can be purchased from the U.S. Geological Survey. Contact your county farm agent if you have difficulty in obtaining maps. Once you discover a turkey, mark that

bird's location on your map, and assign him a number or a name. Then you will know where to find that gobbler during hunting season.

The quickest, easiest way to scout for turkeys in the morning is to drive woods roads and stop and call (with a crow, owl, or hawk call) every 200 or so yards. Each time you get a response, note the turkey's location on your aerial photo or topographical map.

If no roads go through the property you hunt, use some form of identifiable landmark to move across the terrain. If you are hunting mountainous terrain, walk the ridges of each mountain, call from the tops of the ridges, and try to pinpoint the locations of the turkeys you hear gobble. If you are hunting farmland, walk the edges of fields and record where the turkeys are. If you are hunting in flatlands, follow creeks that flow through the woodlots to locate gobblers.

If turkeys do not gobble on their own in the

Topo maps can help you locate ridges where you can expect to find gobblers.

mornings, use your owl call to force them to gobble. After the sun rises, blow crow calls or hawk calls to entice the toms to talk. Once you find a roost site, there's a chance that the same turkey may use the same roost site during the turkey season. When I locate a gobbling turkey, I also mark the compass course I must take to reach his roost site.

## Learn a Turkey's Schedule

Most turkey hunters only scout to help them take gobblers during the first two hours of light in the spring. However, to be a good turkey hunter and to more than double your odds for bagging a bird, you need to know where the turkey goes and what he does all day long. For me, understanding a turkey's daily plan is what hunting is all about.

When you hear a turkey gobble in the morning from the roost, get within 100 to 150 yards of that gobbling bird and listen for him to fly down. If that particular tom is a bird that gobbles often, he usually will gobble in the places where he is feeding and where he meets his hens.

Make every attempt to stay near the bird all day to learn where he goes when he flies down, where he feeds, where he struts, where he dusts (cleans his feathers on the ground), and where he mates. Watch the turkey in the field, notice about what time he leaves the field and where he enters the woods when he leaves the field, information that can be invaluable later in the season. In states that permit all-day hunting, you need to know where the turkey loafs in the middle of the day to dodge the heat, the course he takes back to his roost tree, and about what time he flies into the tree. Besides listening to gobbling turkeys to determine their daily routine, you can use binoculars to watch them. By observing turkeys, you soon will learn which are the dominant tom and the dominant hen.

Another way to determine a turkey's movements is to study the land itself. If you hear a turkey gobbling in a particular section after he flies down from the roost, more than likely this will be a strut zone. Wait until the tom leaves that place before going to where the turkey has been gobbling—usually a clearing, a road or a firebreak. You may be able to see scratch marks on the ground where the turkey has dragged his wings, as well as tracks, droppings and feathers.

Pinpointing where a turkey struts is important. If during hunting season you fail to call up a gobbler when he flies down from his roost, you may be able to move immediately to the strut zone and call the turkey into that site, because that is the place he is going. When a turkey leaves his strut zone, often he will move to a field or an open spot to feed. Since turkeys

**With binoculars, you not only can keep up with turkey movements but also determine the pecking order of the flock.**

**This hunter has located cleared earth with scratchings where the turkey's wing tips scraped the ground.**

With a spotting scope you can remain concealed at a distance and see
where turkeys enter and leave a field.

are creatures of habit, locating the route the
turkey takes from his strut zone to his feeding
area means you can relocate and call the bird to
you from that spot.

The easiest way to bag a turkey is to call him
to you along a route he normally travels each
day. If you do not encounter the gobbler along
the route he takes from his strut zone, learn
where he enters the field or woodlot where he
feeds in the middle of the day. Most of the
time, turkeys will enter and leave their feeding
area by the same route, usually an open place
with good visibility in all directions. Taking a
stand in these regions will increase your
chances of bagging a bird. When a turkey is
feeding, dusting, bugging or mating in an open
field between 11:00 a.m. and 1:00 p.m., the
sun will begin to heat up his feathers, forcing

him back to the woods to cool off. By late
afternoon, when it's cooler, the turkeys may
return to the field and feed before they fly up
to roost.

Generally turkeys like to roost either on high
points of land or in tall trees from where they
can see in all directions. Often turkeys will
walk within 100 yards of the roost tree before
flying up. If you hunt in a state that permits
all-day hunting, and if you know the route the
turkey takes back to his roost tree, you often
can call him to you just before fly-up time.

If you scout for turkeys prior to the season
without a gun or a turkey call, you not only
will learn more about how, where and when to
take them, you will enjoy the sport more. But
be cautious not to spend all your time learning
the whereabouts of only one gobbler. If some-

Turkeys like to roost on high ridges from where they have an unobstructed view of potential predators or on trees overhanging water where they feel safe from land-based predators.

# TURKEY SIGN

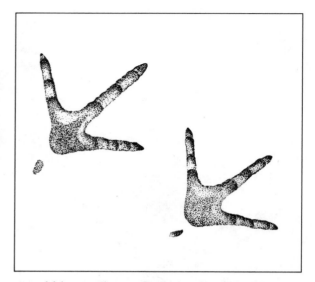

At left are hen droppings. Notice the puddle shape. Gobbler droppings, at right, are more elongated, often shaped like a question mark.

A gobbler track usually has a long middle toe. The three toes of a hen's track are about the same length.

Here's what a group of gobbler tracks would look like on a road after a rainstorm.

one else bags that bird on opening morning, all of your scouting will have been in vain.

Try to learn all you can about at least five or six turkeys prior to the season. Find turkeys well away from roads and easy access places. Then if other hunters have located the turkeys closest to the road, you still will have turkeys to hunt deep in the forest.

Especially if you are hunting public lands, learn to give up the easy turkeys. If you locate a gobbler roosting less than 200 yards from a public road, more than likely every other turkey hunter in that region has found that same gobbler. Assume that someone else will get that turkey on opening day. Pinpoint a turkey deeper in the woods that most other turkey hunters will not locate.

To be a successful scouter, always assume other people are scouting for the same turkeys. Attempt to find gobblers you feel no one else will discover. Only by outscouting other turkey hunters will you consistently bag a gobbler.

## TURKEY SIGN

The droppings of a hen turkey usually are round and puddle-shaped, whereas the droppings of a male turkey are in the shape of a question mark.

A gobbler's track has a longer middle toe than a hen's track. A hen's toes will be about the same length. These tracks are easiest to find on clean ground in fields, roads or firebreaks. The best time to see turkey tracks and to learn how and where turkeys move is immediately after a rain. After an all-night downpour, turkeys will walk in open places to let the wind and the sun dry their feathers. If you drive or walk down a road or along the edge of a field after a rain, you may spot turkey tracks.

Look for scratches in strutting and dusting sites. Strutting sites are usually found in open fields, on roads, or in clear spots. The scratches are made by turkeys dragging their wings in the dirt when they strut. The wing feathers of a gobbler are often broomed or broken off on the ends from strutting; a hen's wing feathers almost always are rounded. Dusting sites are usually located on ground with loose dirt. The turkeys clean their feathers and rid them of parasites by rolling in the loose earth.

You can find a feeding area in the woods by noting where leaves are pushed back and piled up. Turkeys use their feet to uncover worms and nuts. Generally a roost site will be a large tree with a number of turkey droppings around it.

## CALLS FOR SCOUTING

As mentioned previously, when scouting use calls that imitate other birds or animals rather than turkeys. You don't want to call in a tom as yet, merely to locate him. Calls that encourage a tom to talk without coming to you include the owl call, the crow call, the hawk call, the pileated woodpecker call and the coyote howler.

Before sun up, owls begin to hoot and turkeys often gobble in response. When you owl hoot, give one or two hoots. Then be quiet and listen for a gobbler to answer you. Only give one or two hoots, because if a turkey is very vocal in the morning, he may gobble as soon as you hoot. If you give a long series of hoots, you may not be able to hear him gobble while you are calling. If one or two hoots don't elicit a gobble, then make a series of hoots that sound like who-cooks, who-cooks, who-cooks-for-you-all. This sound will produces the most natural hoot that turkeys will answer.

Begin your hooting softly. A turkey may be close by, and you do not want to blow him out of the tree with loud calling. If you do not get a response after you hoot, hoot louder. If you still do not hear a turkey gobble, hoot very loudly. If a turkey still fails to

Strut zones are often found on woods roads. Look for an abundance of tracks with dragmarks of turkeys' wings (see close-up below) on either side.

A dusting site is often found on the edge of a field or a road, or in a bald spot in the woods. Again, look for scratches made by wing tips.

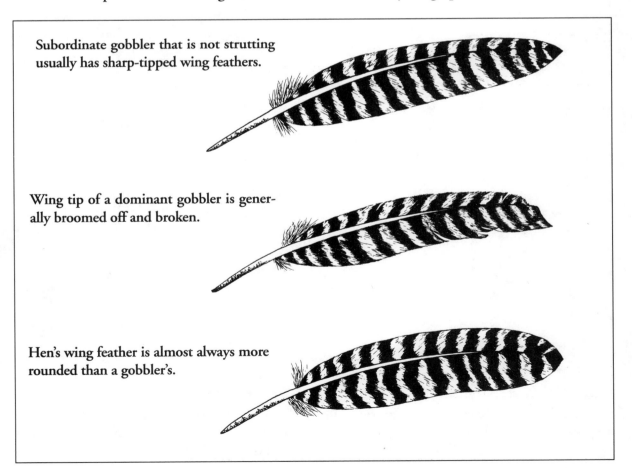

Subordinate gobbler that is not strutting usually has sharp-tipped wing feathers.

Wing tip of a dominant gobbler is generally broomed off and broken.

Hen's wing feather is almost always more rounded than a gobbler's.

respond, move to another spot, and repeat the same routine.

If you are in the woods later in the morning, notice that turkeys will gobble when a crow emits its high-pitched scream. If you fail to get a gobble from a turkey with an owl call, try a crow call later in the morning. Both crow and owl calls can produce a gob-ble at almost any time of the day.

To make a lock-lipped longbeard give away his location, use a hawk call or a pileated woodpecker call, which are high-pitched shrieks many turkeys will answer. Hawk and woodpecker calls are especially effective later in the day. Other sounds that cause turkeys to gobble include jet planes flying overhead, whis-

**Turkeys often gobble early in the morning in response to the hooting of an owl.**

**If you are hunting in the woods later in the morning, notice that turkeys answer crows when they begin to call.**

tles or horns sounding on a highway or at a factory, or loud tugboats moving on a nearby river. Any loud, unusual sound can make a turkey gobble and give away his location. Some turkeys gobble to car doors slamming, chain saws cranking up, school buses hitting potholes, and sirens of passing ambulances. When scouting for turkeys, listen for loud, high-pitched and unusual sounds. You may hear a turkey gobble right after that sound.

By spending the time to scout for turkeys, you will learn to understand the birds better than does the occasional hunter. Scouting and learning the ways of the wild turkey are the essence of true hunting. Squeezing the trigger is just target practice.

Even a lock-lipped longbeard may answer a hawk call and give away his location.

A turkey even gobbles when a jet flies low overhead or when he hears other loud noises.

# 5

# Learning to Call

Turkey hunting is one of the fastest-growing sports in America today, because more and more hunters have learned how to call turkeys. By calling, the hunter actually communicates with a tom and can pinpoint his location, determine or change his mood, or create an imaginary hen that lures him into range.

When you go one-on-one with a gobbler, you have to enter his world, think like he thinks and talk like he talks. In the movie *Patton*, George C. Scott, who plays Patton, stands on a hill, watching the retreat of the tank corps of the famous German general Rommel, and screams, "I've read your book!"

Because Patton had read Rommel's book on strategy, he was able to defeat him during World War II in the African deserts. To beat the smartest strategist in the woods, the wild turkey, you not only have to know what he is thinking and understand where he wants to go, you must carry on a deceptive conversation

with him to bring him within shotgun range.

Early hunters noticed that during the spring when a hen turkey called, often a gobbler would come to her. They learned to produce the sounds of wild turkey hens, so instead of chasing the gobblers they lured the birds to them.

The first turkey caller more than likely used his natural voice. As the sport evolved, hunters learned they could scratch on wood, blow on leaves, and rub sticks and rocks together to make sounds to which gobblers would respond.

You not only must learn to imitate the calls of the wild turkey, you also must know when and how to call. You would never take your girlfriend to a quiet restaurant where the lights are low, the music soft, and the atmosphere romantic, look into her eyes and then scream at the top of your lungs, "I want to marry you!" You wouldn't walk up to your next-door neighbor in his backyard, peer over his shoulder as

The hen turkey clucks to say, "I'm over here."

A young gobbler *kee-kees* before he can learn to gobble.

Male turkeys gobble for many reasons: to attract hens, to demonstrate their dominance, and in reaction to different sounds in the woods.

you spot large billows of smoke pouring from his upstairs window, and whisper in a low, calm voice, "James, your house is on fire."

In calling turkeys, as in everyday life, your language and feeling must be appropriate to the situation. Following are the most common sounds made by wild turkeys. Each one has its own particular rhythm and feeling which you should try to capture.

## TURKEY CALLS

### The Cluck

When a hen gets excited, either because of danger approaching or seeing movement she cannot identify, she clucks. If she hears a gobbler sound off, and she is very excited and ready to breed, she clucks insistently. This sound is called "cutting." If the hen is frightened, she gives an alarm cluck. Even though only one, short, crisp sound is made, that sound can communicate many different moods and feelings.

The gobbler also clucks. His clucks often are more raspy than the hen's. Sometimes he clucks to let other turkeys know where he is or when he sees something he does not understand. Immediately before a tom runs off, he clucks differently and makes a sound called a "putt." The emotion and the rhythm of the call determine what the bird is trying to say more than the sound itself.

## The Purr

The purr is a low, guttural sound hens usually make when they are feeding. This is a sound hunters make to calm down a tom when he gets too excited. When a hen purrs, she is like a woman humming. She is merely contented. However, when gobblers purr with feeling, it is one of the most aggressive sounds they make. This type of purr is known as the "fighting purr." Although the sounds are similar in name and tone, often the volume and speed with which the sounds are made and the emotion they attempt to communicate carry different messages to the birds.

## The Yelp

The yelp, one of the most common turkey sounds, carries many messages. The yelp can be compared to someone talking to himself—a very contented, noisy call with no intent to communicate. Older hens often yelp in the fall to call a scattered flock together. This form of yelping, which is known as the "assembly call," expresses excitement.

The yelp also can be an excited mating call, sometimes called "cackling," that the hen uses to tell the gobbler she is in the mood to breed and is on the way to meet him. The hen can make this same call to say, "Hey, big boy, I'm over here at my house. If you want to have a romantic encounter with me, you've got to come to where I am."

Another form of yelping hens and gobblers employ is to tell each other where they are in the woods and to say, "I've found some good groceries over here. If you want to eat, come on over."

In the morning when hen turkeys first wake up, they give a series of low, light yelps, much like a yawn. This "tree calling," as it is known, says, "I'm up in this tree, and I'm awake. I haven't really decided to fly down yet. But when I do, I'll let you know where I am."

Young gobblers have a difficult time at first trying to yelp. Because their voice boxes are not fully developed and they are not sure how to make the sound, their voices pop and crack, much like a teenager whose voice is changing. In attempting to yelp, young gobblers make a *kee-kee* sound. This form of yelping is called the "kee-kee run" or the "squealing call." Turkeys combine these sounds into a complex language inflected by feeling and rhythm.

## The Gobble

The gobble is made by the male turkey and is used in several ways. The turkey gobbles primarily to tell hens where he is so they can come to him to be bred. An older turkey gobbles to demonstrate his dominance and to let younger male birds know he is the supreme turkey and claims the right to breed all the hens in the area. When an older, dominant bird gobbles, the subordinate male birds usually stop.

A turkey also gobbles in reaction to different sounds in the woods. Often these sounds are high-pitched like the call of a pileated woodpecker. Turkeys gobble to the sound of jet airplanes passing overhead or car doors slamming, called "shock gobbling." Some believe this gobble signifies surprise.

## Drumming

Gobblers make a drumming sound that is like the noise of an eighteen wheeled truck starting up a steep grade when the driver revs his engine; then, as the truck begins to slow, he shifts gears to make the pull easier. The sound is similar to *p-t-t-t-vroom*. This is a very excited mating call. Many older toms which have learned that gobbling lures in hunters as well as hens may resort to drumming. Learn to recognize this sound.

## The Scratch

Another sound turkeys make is scratching in the leaves as they search for food. Other turkeys often come when they hear this sound, much like a farmhand who knows the sound of the dinner bell means lunch is being served.

## Wings Brushing

Another very subtle sound turkeys make is the noise of their wings brushing against the sides of trees and bushes as they walk through the woods. You can use this sound to mask your own movement through the woods.

## Flying Noises

Turkeys also make noise when they fly. When a turkey flies up or down from the roost, the other turkeys in the area know what that sound means. This sound may trigger the same action by other individuals in the flock.

## THE BOX CALL

In the early 1900s, hunters discovered they

**A young gobbler makes a drumming sound when he struts.**

Turkeys scratch in the leaves to find food.

You can hear the sound of turkeys' wings beating the air when they fly to and from the roost.

could whittle a box out of wood and attach a paddle to the end of the box to produce the calls of the wild turkey. During this time, several enterprising sportsmen began to make and sell turkey calls and they taught hunters how to use them. For instance, M.L. Lynch of Homewood, Alabama, the founder of Lynch Game Calls, traveled the South like a revival preacher, stood on street corners, and used his box calls to draw crowds and sell his products. Lynch taught thousands of hunters how to call turkeys.

A thin-walled wooden box with a paddle lid attached to one end, the box call produces a sound when you slide the lid across the side of the box. The side and the lid are chalked, and the friction created by these two chalked surfaces coming into contact with each other can make all the calls of the wild turkey. Some boxes have two calling surfaces. A double-sided box is encircled with rubber bands so that when you shake it back and forth the lid produces the sound of a gobble. To produce a yelp, slide the lid across the side of the box with one sweeping stroke. To make a cluck, strike the lid against the side of the box with one quick, popping stroke. Making several fast clucks in quick succession produces the cutting call. To produce a purr, pull the lid across the side of the box lightly and slowly.

To produce the maximum amount of sound

To protect a box call in foul weather, store it in a plastic bag.

**The box call, one of the first turkey calls developed, was originally whittled from wood.**

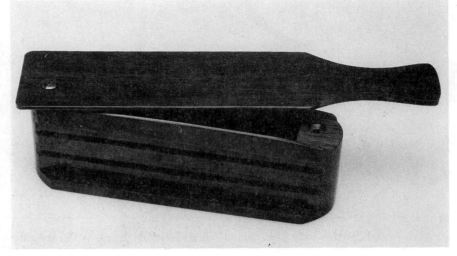

from a box, hold the lid of the box perpendicular to the ground and strike the lid sharply with the side of the box, which will increase the volume and make the call seem to pop. Until the last twenty years, the box call was the most frequently used device to call in gobblers.

## THE PUSHBUTTON BOX CALL

This simplest of all calls requires only that you push a peg with your finger to produce a hen call. With this call, you can cluck by simply tapping the end of the peg with the palm of your hand. Produce yelps by pushing the peg three or four times in succession. You can cut by utilizing the palm of your hand to pat the peg in rapid succession. Push the peg slowly and gently with your finger to make a purr.

The pushbutton call can be taped to the forearm of your shotgun. Then you can operate the call and hold your gun at the same time. This call is deadly on toms and currently is being used by many of the nation's leading turkey hunters.

**With a pushbutton call it is easy to mimic the clucking of a hen or the yelp of a gobbler.**

**The pushbutton call can be taped or velcroed to the barrel of your shotgun and operated by a string.**

## THE FRICTION CALL

The original friction call was made from a piece of slate whose surface was roughed with sandpaper. The hunter formed a sound chamber by cupping his hand around the slate and scratched a wooden peg across the surface, producing the sound of a wild turkey hen. However, forming the proper sound chamber to get a true turkey sound often was difficult. In later years, the slate was encased in a box that created the sound chamber. The box had a hole in the bottom. The sportsman scratched the surface of the slate as he had done before and the sound came through the hole. Today plastic and even aluminum are fast replacing slate and wood for box calls.

Most friction calls work on the principle that to produce the sound, you move a striker across the surface of the call. To cluck, you simply make one short, sharp strike on the surface of the friction call. You produce the cut by making several fast clucks. Hold the striker like a pencil pointing toward you, and make small, circular motions to produce a yelp. For a purr, make a light cluck on the call with the striker, and then continue to draw the striker across the surface.

## THE MOUTH DIAPHRAGM CALL

In the late 1920s, a rabid dog was indirectly responsible for producing today's most popular call—the mouth diaphragm. Jim Radcliff, Jr., of Andalusia, Alabama, was in New Orleans being treated for rabies when he met a street entertainer who made bird calls with a "diaphram" in his mouth. Radcliff worked with the street entertainer to modify and change the diaphragm call, which was made of a horseshoe-shaped piece of lead and a thin piece of latex rubber, to sound like the call of the wild turkey.

Today the lead horseshoe of the diaphragm turkey call has been replaced by lightweight aluminum, thinner pieces of latex are used, and

New friction calls are made of plastic or aluminum. To produce a call, you move the striker across the surface.

**Diaphragm call fits in the roof of the mouth. It is one of the most difficult calls to learn to use.**

dropping the jaw as the air passes over the rubber reed, you can make a yelp. To purr, which is the most difficult call to create on a diaphragm, make sure your lips are moist, then blow out while vibrating your tongue and lips up and down.

The pitch and the tone of the diaphragm call are determined not only by the amount of air passed over the reed and the force with which the call is blown but also by the number of latex reeds used to make the call and whether or not the reeds are split. The more reeds in a call, the deeper and coarser the sound. The

the body of the call is covered with fabric or plastic tape.

To use the diaphragm call, place it in the roof of your mouth, and with your tongue, meter air over the latex rubber to produce turkey sounds. The amount and frequency of the air blown over the rubber reed determines the kind of call produced.

To cluck with this call, put your lips together, blow out a short, sharp burst of air, and smack your lips at the same time. To cut on a diaphragm call, make a rapid series of clucks. By metering air over the diaphragm and

**When using a diaphragm call, most hunters cup their hand near their mouth to make a sound chamber for better resonance.**

split reed also makes the call more raspy.

The diaphragm is the most difficult call to learn to use. You must seat the call properly in the roof of your mouth, position the tip of your tongue in the proper place on the reed and learn just how much air produces the different sounds of the wild turkey. The best way to learn to use the diaphragm call is to listen to an audio cassette. Put the call in the roof of your mouth, and then try to say the word "shoot" while blowing air over your tongue and vibrating the reed.

Not only does the diaphragm mouth call realistically produce the sound of both hens and gobblers, it also gives you the advantage of hands-free operation and little or no movement when you are attempting to bring a gobbler within gun range. If a gobbler veers to the right or to the left when he is just out of range, you can call softly to the bird using the diaphragm and cause him to turn and come to you. If you need to make a tom quit strutting and stick his neck up to enable you to get a shot, you do not have to move with a diaphragm call to give a cluck or a yelp. If a hen calls to a gobbler in front of you and tries to pull the tom away from you, without moving you can call that gobbler back with a diaphragm call.

A problem associated with any kind of turkey call is that particular types of calls—whether diaphragm or friction—all speak with the same voice. To change your voice you must change your calls. Carrying a backpack full of box calls or slate calls through the woods is cumbersome, but you can take five to twenty diaphram calls with you in a small pouch in your shirt pocket. Then you can change calls and voices quickly and easily.

## THE GOBBLING CALL

Although most hunters use box calls to gobble, the Red Wolf Gobbling Tube also is very effective in making turkeys shock gobble. However, when a hunter uses this gobbling call, he makes the sounds other hunters are hunting. This call can be dangerous and is not recommended for use on public hunting lands. It should be used only on private hunting lands and with extreme caution.

## OTHER CALLS

Some hunters of yesteryear cut a hole in the bottom of a small snuff can, cut half the lid away and stretched latex rubber over the hole in the lid leaving a small opening through which air could pass. By blowing air over the rubber, they could make loud and often raspy turkey calls. These calls are still used.

The wingbone call originally was made from two bones in the turkey's wing. The bones were glued together to form a small pipe around 6 to 7 inches in length and about ¼ inch in diameter. To produce clucks and yelps, hunters sucked on the wingbone. Sucking small puffs of air through the wingbone call produced a cluck, while longer, faster puffs of air sucked through the call made the yelping sound of a hen turkey.

As discussed earlier other calls that can cause turkeys to gobble include owl hooters, pileated woodpecker calls, hawk calls, coyote howlers and crow calls.

Most turkey hunters agree that to hunt the wild turkey successfully, you must be able to use several types of calls. On any given day, a gobbler will come to one call when he will not respond to another.

Remember, though, a little calling goes a long way when you are talking turkey to a tom. You do not have to be a master of all the calls to enjoy the sport of turkey hunting and be successful. If you can produce a cluck and a yelp on any one of the calls, you can call in a gobbler.

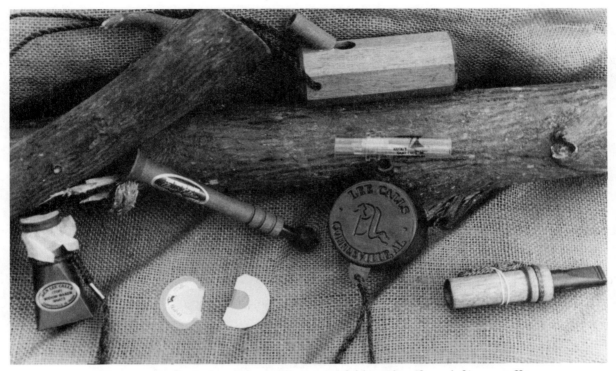

Many types of wind-operated calls are available today (from left): a snuff can, a tube-type call; a wingbone call (top); two diaphragm calls (bottom); a M.L. Lynch owl hooter (top); a pileated woodpecker call (middle); a Ben Lee owl hooter (bottom); a crow call.

## HOW TO IMPROVE YOUR CALLING

Practicing correctly will improve your skill, but practicing incorrectly will not help your calling ability and even may decrease its effectiveness. To learn to call correctly, listen to cassette tapes available from many manufacturers of turkey calls. These are recordings of master turkey callers. Also, attend turkey calling contests and record the calls of the best contestants. Then try to imitate them. Next, tape-record your own calls. Play both tapes and listen how closely you've imitated the calls of the masters. Carry your tape recorder with you into the woods, and record the calls the wild turkey makes in the spring. There is no better teacher anywhere than the wild turkey. Attempt to combine the sounds of turkeys in the wild and the sounds of the contest. Often when I have recorded master turkey callers and then listened to the tape, I have realized that my calls are too fast or too loud or have improper rhythm.

A method to improve your calling that I recommend highly is to take your recorder to an area in the woods where you have spotted turkeys before, set it up in a tree, move away 100 yards, and start your calls. This way, you'll record both your own calls and those made by turkeys. You may learn when you replay the tape that you are calling much too loud with a diaphragm caller. You may not have realized this from practicing indoors.

Also to improve your calling, find a tame turkey. Few turkeys or turkey hunters can distinguish between the calls of a tame turkey and a wild turkey. Listen to tame turkeys, and attempt to imitate their conversations.

Be sure the call you are using fits you. Just because a diaphragm call is built a certain way and has a specified amount of tape on it does not mean the call will fit your mouth. You may need to trim quite a bit of tape off your mouth call to get it to fit better. You may not be able to make the sound you want because you have not been matched with the best call for you.

This applies not only to diaphragm calls but also to slate calls. The design of many slate calls requires you to move the peg in circles to produce the right sound. On other calls, a half circle will do. On some calls, a back-and-forth motion is needed to yield the best call. The lids on a box call are meant to slide across the side of the box without being forced or having any pressure applied to them. The lid of a quality box caller then should slide back across the box without making any sound. Be certain you know what to do with your call and that the call fits you.

## STRATEGIES FOR CALLING

A gobbler has been asleep all night and has had wild dreams about beautiful hens and exciting times. His testosterone level is extremely high. As soon as he wakes up, he is ready to breed. The first thing he does is begin to call a list of his girlfriends. Although most may answer him, not all are ready for an early-morning encounter. So he has to find one in the right mood.

If you hear a turkey gobble in the morning,

**When a turkey wakes up in the morning, the first thing he does is call his girlfriends for a date. The hunter then tries to imitate a hen.**

answer him quickly with a series of yelps. If even before you finish giving three or four yelps he gobbles the second time, then you know that turkey is very excited and eager to meet his hen immediately. You can call back to him with some cackles that say, "Okay, big boy, I know you're over there.  Come on over here, and we will have a romantic interlude."

If the turkey gobbles again, he is more than likely to come toward you in a hurry. Continue to call him excitedly until he flies out of the tree and hits the ground. Then you better have your gun up and be ready to shoot.

This same turkey may respond differently on another morning after he gobbles. When you answer him with hen calls, he may wait from one to five minutes before he gobbles again, which indicates he is not very excited about mating.   Call to this bird calmly and infrequently with light yelps and purrs. Do not talk to the tom any more than he talks to you. By matching the emotional level of your calling to his gobbles you are more likely to pull him in than if you try to change his mood. The most productive way to call a turkey to you is to duplicate his mood. If that fails, try to change his mood.

Have you ever noticed high school football players on the beach? They strut, showing off their muscles and their manhood, especially if a good-looking girl is sunbathing in a bikini nearby. Usually this girl gets her guy not by initiating the conversation or letting him know in any way she is interested in him but rather by casually glancing at him every now and then or simply ignoring him altogether. Often this offends the young man's ego and forces him to prove he is more desirable than she thinks.

The same tactic will work when you are trying to pull a gobbler into gun range. Often-

**If a turkey gobbles in answer to your calls, you know he is very excited and may come to you. Try to match the excitement of his gobbles.**

**As the gobbler moves closer, he struts proudly and gobbles more frequently.**

times when a turkey gobbles, struts and drums, he believes the lure of his beautiful feathers and the sound of his masculine voice are enough to attract a coquettish hen. All the rules of nature dictate that the hen goes to the gobbler. When the hen does not come, the turkey moves towards her and begins to strut and gobble even more. But instead of matching his mood by giving excited calls, you will be wise to calm the situation by acting like a girl on the beach who pretends she's more interested in making sandcastles than flirting with a boy. Give soft clucks, yelps or purrs like a contented hen, or simply scratch in the leaves. Pretend you are a hen uninterested in mating. When the gobbler hears these contented sounds, often he will calm down and change his tactics. He may stop strutting and gobbling and approach quietly. When he comes within shotgun range, you can take him.

Some gobblers do not want to expend any energy to mate with a hen. They prefer to have the hen come to them. If you encounter such a reluctant gobbler, you have to change his mood and get him so excited he'll come to you. You must build the emotional level of your calling. After giving a few yelps and determining the turkey is not going to come to you, give some excited cuts and cackles. If a sequence of calls fails to produce a bird, use two or three different types of calls, such as the diaphragm, the box and the slate, to speak with different voices. Then you can sound like three or four different hens that are all excited, ready to breed and telling the gobbler to come to them, which will be more pressure than most gobblers can stand. His sexual mood will be raised, and his desire will be intensified.

If cutting and cackling with several different calls fails to move the tom, the final step is to challenge his manhood. After a series of loud, excited cuts and cackles with various calls, then

If you locate a gobbler that is in the company of some hens, he may be difficult to call since he's already occupied.

gobble—after looking in all directions to be sure you are not gobbling in front of another hunter. That tom may think that another gobbler has moved in on his harem and may move in to challenge him.

## WHEN NOT TO CALL

The most important factor in effective calling is knowing when not to call. Many hunters overcall turkeys. The most productive calling is the least amount of calling that will elicit a response. The purpose of all calling is to get a bird to come to you. Once you have a bird moving toward you, usually you do not need to continue to call except in isolated instances.

A true turkey hunter wants to make the turkey hunt him. At a certain point in a successful turkey hunt, you change your strategy from being the hunter to becoming the hunted. To bring a tom in close enough to take a shot, you must give that turkey reason to find you. Once you have called the gobbler, have determined his emotional level, and either matched or changed it, talk to him as little as possible.

If you have ever watched turkeys in the woods, notice they walk very slowly most of the time. A turkey's stride is usually less than 12 inches. If you call to a turkey 100 yards away and that bird is walking naturally toward you, it may take him thirty minutes to an hour to reach you. If that gobbler is not very excited, he may take even longer.

When you determine the turkey is coming to you, quit calling. If you do call, make your calls infrequent, very soft and short. Often if I believe I have a gobbler coming to me, and I think he may not know exactly where I am, I

**When you are learning to use a turkey call, the entire family may suffer from your incessant practicing—but don't let them deter you.**

very carefully and slowly slide my hand down to the ground and scratch in the leaves to let the turkey know where I am but not excite him so much he stops coming.

Patience, more than a lot of calling, will give you a shot at a turkey. Most novice turkey hunters call too much and sit still too little.

Effective turkey hunters call very little and sit in one place for a long time. Although our society teaches that the faster you go, the more you get, in turkey hunting, the reverse is true. The slower you go, and the less you move, the greater are your odds for bagging a bird in most situations.

# 6

# Hunting Spring Turkeys

During the spring of the year, a young man's and a young gobbler's fancies both turn to love. Mother Nature in her infinite wisdom has chosen the most beautiful time of the year for the courtship of both humans and birds.

Unlike humans, the tom turkey has only about six weeks to court, breed and reproduce. At this time of the year, he becomes very aggressive and usually chases hens with a vengeance. Young birds sometimes let their sex drives supersede their survival instincts, but older birds are more cautious. When a gobbler talks, not only are the hens supposed to listen, they are supposed to come on the run to get bred. In the natural order of things, hens go to a tom when he gobbles. When a hunter calls in an attempt to bring a gobbler to him, he asks that gobbler to perform an unnatural act.

Young and inexperienced toms will violate the laws of nature to go to a receptive hen. Older gobblers, which have had more hunter encounters, will wait for a hen to come to them. The male turkey has learned he then can stay out of harm's way.

## SCOUTING

The key to taking a gobbler in the spring is to know where he won't go. Probably every wild critter at some time will break one of the rules they are not suppose to break. However, there are certain rules most gobblers rarely violate.

1) Turkeys do not like to cross water to come to you. Although I have seen turkeys wade sloughs, fly across creeks and even large rivers, generally a gobbler will not cross water if he can help it. If you know where the streams and gullies are, you have a decided advantage when you begin to call a turkey. If a tom gobbles on the other side of water, your best chance of bagging that bird is to cross the water and call from his side.

2) A turkey usually won't move across a ditch, a hill or a valley to come to you. Pinpoint the ditches, hills and valleys in the region where you are hunting. If you can call the turkey from the same hill he is on, he is more likely to respond to you than if you call him across a valley or a ditch. Or, you can begin your calling from the top of a hill and call from

When the gobbler talks, not only do the hens listen, but they come to him to get bred.

Finding a strut zone is an important lead when you're scouting for spring gobblers.

These hunters have found two turkey feathers—a reliable sign that birds are in the area.

the ridges rather than from the valleys. Turkeys prefer to walk uphill rather than downhill. Also your calls will carry farther from the hilltops than they will from the valleys.

3) Turkeys prefer to walk in open woods because they know that predators usually lurk in thickets. If you hear a turkey call on the other side of a thicket your best chance of bagging that bird is to get around the thicket so it's no longer a barrier between you and the turkey.

4) A turkey can duck under or fly over a fence, but usually he won't. Once again, if you hear a turkey gobble, your best chance to get that bird to come to you is to be on his side of the fence.

## SETTING UP ON SPRING TURKEYS

The term "setting up" means choosing the spot to sit and call turkeys. Picking the best place from which to call is important. If you select a site the turkey will not come to, then all your calling will be fruitless.

When considering a place to set up on a gobbler, walk through the woods and keep looking behind you for a big tree in a clearing. By selecting a tree that's behind you, you see what the gobbler will see when he comes to you. Generally, look for a tree that's wider than your shoulders but not necessarily the biggest tree in the area. The largest tree stands out, and a turkey tends to notice it first and may spot you. Make sure no thick cover is around the tree, and pick a place where you can see at least thirty or forty yards in all directions. As soon as you spot a turkey, you will have only a few seconds before you can shoot. The longer you can see a turkey, the more time he has to spot you.

One of the worst places I ever took a stand was in the middle of a dirt road. My hunting companion, Bo Pitman, and I had hunted turkeys all morning. At 10:00 a.m., we were walking a woods line owling and trying to make a tom talk. When Pitman hooted, a gob-

**Turkeys like to walk in open woods where they can see a predator approach.**

Although a turkey can duck under a fence, he usually prefers to fly over it.

Do not set up by the biggest tree in the area, which a turkey is apt to notice first, but choose a smaller one that is wider than your shoulders.

This well-camouflaged hunter has found the ideal set-up—a large tree with good visibility on each side and in front.

Eddie Salter, two-time world-champion turkey caller, working a box call behind a blind.

bler sounded less than thirty yards away. If we moved at all, the bird would see us. We quickly sat down in the middle of the road with no cover and called the tom. Luckily a small, rolling hill was in front of us. Speedily the gobbler came in but he spotted us just as he topped the hill. Before he could putt and run, I fired. The bird tumbled. Seldom would you be able to take a bird from such a bad position.

## WOODSMANSHIP

A proficient turkey hunter who knows the land and understands the turkeys on that property can pick the best spot to set up and never have to call to the turkey to take him. Experienced turkey hunters use the term "woodsmanship" quite fre-

quently. Often you will hear hunters say, "Woodsmanship bags more turkeys than calling." But what does the term "woodsmanship" really mean when applied to turkey hunting? Well, I would define a good woodsman as follows:

He knows everything about the terrain—where turkeys feed, water, roost, loaf, strut, cross roads and enter and leave fields.

He knows how to walk through the woods slowly and quietly.

He studies turkeys and knows where a turkey will not go, when to call, and when to be quiet. He understands the importance of patience in turkey hunting.

He is a student of nature. He learns how to blend in and become a part of the woods rather than being an alien in the environment.

Brad Harris, of Neosho, Missouri, finds that his woodsmanship is often more important in bagging gobblers than his calling ability.

A good woodsman can walk quietly through the woods without spooking animals or birds.

## BEGINNING THE HUNT

A turkey hunt begins when a tom gobbles. On most warm, bluebird days, a turkey will start to gobble on his own before daylight. Many hunters go into the woods and owl call immediately to make a turkey gobble. However, I prefer to wait until sunrise. If a turkey gobbles on his own, then he usually is excited and will respond readily to your call. Probably some owls in the area will be hooting anyway.

If the bird does not gobble on his own just before first light, I will owl hoot to persuade the tom to talk. Once the turkey gobbles, you must determine his whereabouts. Usually I let a turkey gobble two or three times before I approach him. Then I am sure which way the bird is facing.

Knowing which direction the turkey is looking when he gobbles is critical in determining his location. If the turkey is looking away from you when he gobbles, he will sound much farther away than he really is. If you do not know the turkey is looking away from you when he gobbles, you run the risk of getting too close to him and possibly spooking him off the roost. If you know the turkey is facing you when he gobbles, then you can take a stand, set up farther away from him, and be less likely to spook him.

Once you pinpoint the bird's location and determine what direction he is facing, then try to get closer. If you can get between 100 and 150 yards from a turkey and take a stand next to a big tree in fairly open woods, you will be ready to begin calling.

Before you start to call, clear all sticks and leaves away from the base of the tree to avoid making noise. Don't leave a lot of bare ground. Just clear away enough brush so you can move

**If a turkey gobbles on his own, you will have a better chance to take him than if you have to call to make him gobble.**

around the tree without snapping twigs or rustling leaves. If possible, cut a few small bushes and set them in front of you to break up your silhouette, or use a portable blind. If the turkey already is on the ground or you hear him fly down before you get your blind built, sit next to the tree quickly, and forget about the blind.

How you sit on a turkey stand determines how long you can remain motionless. I never sit on my leg for fear it will go to sleep and tingle. Then I will have to move.

In the early years of my turkey hunting, I took a stand one morning and folded my leg under me. Although this position was comfortable for awhile, as the bird began to come in, I felt my leg going to sleep. Because I wanted to

Proper position on a turkey stand—back against tree, knees up, shotgun resting on knees.

take the bird, I remained still and concentrated all my attention on the turkey. My patience finally paid off. When the bird was at twenty-two yards, I fired, and he tumbled. Immediately I jumped up to retrieve the bird, but my now-numb leg would not support my weight. I fell flat on my face. Falling down was bad enough, but not being able to get up was much worse. To get to the bird in a hurry, I had to crawl through flooded timber, acquiring plenty of mud along the way. I learned a great lesson—do not sit on your leg when you are turkey hunting.

The proper position is to sit square on your seat facing the turkey sound, knees bent in front of you and shotgun resting on your knee. You can sit in this position comfortably for some time. If you do have to make minor adjustments as the turkey comes in, you can move easily from this position.

## CALLING SPRING TURKEYS

### Turkeys on the Roost

Once you are in position, and the turkey is gobbling, begin by giving some tree calls. These are very soft, light yelps the hen turkey makes in a tree before she flies down to mate. If the gobbler answers the hen's calling immediately, you may not have to make any more calls. If you hear the turkey fly down, he may fly directly to your stand. However, if he does not come straight to you when he flies down, give a few yelps. Listen for the turkey to respond. If he gobbles back and you hear him moving toward you, do not call again.

The purpose of calling is to make the turkey come to you. Once he starts moving to you, get ready to shoot. Point your gun in the direction you expect the turkey to come from, and wait. Pick a landmark at thirty yards, such as a couple of trees. When the turkey passes those trees, shoot. Otherwise, hold your fire. Many old-timers cluck three times and throw their calls away to make sure they do not overcall the bird—one of the novice hunter's mistakes. This tactic often will produce best on private lands with turkeys that have not been under severe hunting pressure. The more turkeys are hunted, the more calling you may have to do.

If you are hunting later in the season or on public lands, you may want to use more sneaky techniques and more sophisticated calling. On public lands, the quicker you can get a tom to come to you, the better your chances are for bagging him.

A more aggressive form of calling is to take a stand and give a tree call. Once the turkey answers, wait about five minutes and give a fly-down cackle, a series of fast, excited clucks followed by excited yelps. As soon as you make the fly-down cackle, pat the side of your leg with your gloved hand to simulate the beating of the wings of the hen as she flies down. Wait about two minutes. Then begin to cut, a series of fast clucks that denote excitement and the willingness of the hen to breed. Often this series of calls will seem to snatch a gobbler off the limb. Because he may run to you, be ready for the shot. If the gobbler is slow in coming to you, you can continue to cut until the bird is close enough to see you. Then stop your calling, and prepare to shoot.

Aggressive calling often brings in a gobbler within fifty yards—but then he stops and begins to strut and drum, expecting the hen to come to him. Three strategies may work if a turkey hangs up:

Quit calling altogether. The turkey either will stop strutting and drumming and come to you or he will walk away.

Scratch in the leaves and purr like an uninterested hen. This may lure the gobbler closer so the "hen" can see him and come to mate.

Give soft yelps when the turkey drops his

**When calling to a turkey on his roost, keep your calls soft and infrequent.**

strut to let him know you still are in the area. However, as long as a tom is gobbling and coming to you, do not call. Remember, a turkey walks very slowly through the woods. More than likely, the bird will require more time to get to you than you think he will. Be patient.

### Turkeys on the Ground

If you do not find a gobbler until after the birds have flown down, take a stand about 100 yards from the turkey. Remember, when a turkey is on the ground, the woods absorb most of his gobbles. When you hear him, he will sound much farther away than when he gobbles from a tree. Do not set up as close to the turkey as when he's gobbling from a tree. Most of the time, when you hear a turkey gobble on the ground clearly and distinctly, he is close enough for you to call immediately.

Call to the turkey the same way he calls to you. If the turkey gobbles as soon as he hears you call, then call frequently to the bird, possibly as much as once every two to three minutes until you know he is coming to you. If the turkey waits from fifteen seconds to one minute before responding, answer in like manner. If the turkey gobbles excitedly and double or triple gobbles, match his mood with cuts and cackles.

Most turkey hunters either stay too long in a calling position or leave too quickly. Knowing when to go and when to stay is a critical key to successful turkey hunting. As long as a turkey is coming to you or answering your calls, stay where you are. When the tom starts moving away from you and is out of sight, then move, try to get ahead of the turkey, change calls, and call the bird again.

When a turkey quits gobbling, many hunters assume he has left the area. Generally the opposite is true. When a tom stops gobbling, usually he is coming to you. He may move in silently and suddenly appear. When a turkey stops gobbling, I wait a full forty-five minutes before I leave my calling position. Before you learn when to stay and when to go, you probably will spook several turkeys because you leave too quickly.

## TAKING THE SHOT

If you shoot too quickly, you will miss the gobbler. If you wait too long, the bird will see you, and you will not get a shot. Knowing when to shoot makes the difference between success or failure. I decide when to shoot by applying these rules:

Do not shoot if a turkey is more than thirty yards away, even if your gun has a range of forty-five yards. If the turkey does not come into that thirty-yard range, he wins the first round of the contest. If you are shooting a 20-gauge or a blackpowder shotgun, wait until the bird is twenty-five yards away. Although I have killed turkeys ten steps from the tree, these were lucky shots. Usually at this range the shot pattern will not have time to open up and cover the target. Most veteran turkey hunters will tell you that the closer the turkey, the greater your chances of missing the bird.

Never take a shot when you do not have a clear path to the turkey's head and neck. If a blade of grass, a tree or a bush is between me and the turkey's head and neck, I will not shoot. The spinal column and skull of the turkey are very small. Any obstruction can collect the lead intended for the turkey's head and you may miss the bird.

Do not shoot a turkey in the strut. When a turkey is in the strut, his head and neck are coiled back into his feathers and he presents a smaller target. To break a tom out of the strut, all you have to do is cluck. The bird usually will drop his strut, stick his head up and give you a clean shot.

Do not shoot at a running turkey unless you are sure you can hit him. The chances of miss-

If you hear a turkey fly down from his roost, he may fly straight toward your stand. Once he approaches you, cease calling and get ready to shoot.

Never shoot at a turkey when there are obstructions that conceal his head.

Two gobblers in the midst of strutting, their tail feathers fanned. Often cutting and calling aggressively will prompt a gobbler to stop and strut.

ing or injuring the bird are greatly increased.

Do not rush the shot. Often a hunter thinks, "If I don't take this shot, I'm not going to get another." But if a turkey does not present a good shot, do not take it. Let him walk off. Then either try to call him back, set up on him in another place, or hunt him another day. If you shoot and miss, you have educated that gobbler, which will make him more difficult to hunt.

A young spring gobbler like a jake or a two year-old bird can be relatively easy to take. But an older gobbler that has had several hunter encounters can drive you nuts. Since turkeys in the spring want to breed, sex is your ally.

Although some turkeys are easy to call and bag, the more hunting pressure turkeys have experienced, the more difficult they will be to take. The keys to success are careful scouting, skilled calling, and patience.

Do not be discouraged when a tom beats you. Turkeys win more than hunters do. Even the best turkey hunters are defeated some of the time. Spring turkey hunting is exciting because every morning you have an opportunity to test your skills and knowledge against one of the smartest creatures in the woods.

# 7

# Hunting Fall Turkeys

The longbeards of the fall are the most difficult turkeys to bag at any time of the year, but the jakes, which are less than a year old, are easy to take.

The strategy for taking fall turkeys is completely different from that used in the spring. Sex is no longer important to the gobblers. The birds already have passed through their mating cycles, and the hens have made their nests, laid their eggs, and reared their young. Fall calling and

**Jakes are gobblers less than a year old. They are easy to deceive.**

During the fall of the year in some parts of the country, turkeys often have to dig through the snow to find food.

In winter, livestock are often the key to finding gobblers feeding on undigested grain in manure.

hunting tactics are based primarily on the social order of turkeys more than on their sex drive.

The woods also have changed. No longer does the hunter have the lush green foliage of spring for concealment. In many areas of the country, snow covers the ground. Fall hunters often wear different camo patterns. Here is a look at the fall world of the turkey.

During the fall, the turkey's primary diet is nuts and seeds. Often the birds have to scratch through snow to find food. One of the best areas in which to locate turkeys in the fall is around livestock, because livestock face the same problem as turkeys do—finding food.

In the far North when snow covers the ground during turkey season, often you will see turkeys on the pastures of a dairy farm. When dairy farmers clean out their heated barns and spread manure on their pastures, this manure is warmer than the snow. The manure has undigested grain in it that is easy for the turkeys to find and eat. Contact a dairy farmer when you are scouting for fall turkeys.

Ranchers who produce beef cattle also put out hay and grain for their animals during the fall. These food sources for the livestock also contain small seeds and grain on which the turkeys feed.

In the South where turkey hunting is permitted in the fall, look for squirrels when you are hunting. Squirrels feed on many of the same seeds, acorns, dogwood berries and other mast crops that wild turkeys eat. Once you pinpoint a hardwood area with a heavy squirrel concentration, you usually will find a productive place to hunt turkeys.

Many turkey hunters hunt squirrels in the fall to scout for turkeys before the season opens. While walking along rivers and creeks, and bagging bushytails, they look for turkey feathers, droppings and scratchings and hope to see some turkeys as well. Once the squirrel hunters determine where the turkeys are ranging, they know where to begin their search for

the longbeards when the season arrives.

Because turkeys travel some distances in the fall, flocks can leave numbers of tracks. By examining these tracks, a skilled woodsman can determine their age, the flock's direction of travel, and whether it is composed of males and/or females.

## WHY HAVE A FALL SEASON?

Although you may think some states do not have a fall season because of too small a turkey population, the reasons are usually not that simple. Certain states regulate their seasons to control their flocks; other states rely on tradition.

For example, Alabama, my home state, has one of the largest turkey flocks in the nation. However, only twelve of its sixty-seven counties have a fall turkey season. Why? Tradition. About thirty-three states now have fall turkey seasons, compared to forty-nine states that have spring seasons for turkeys.

We all know the Pilgrims and the Indians celebrated Thanksgiving in the fall with a turkey dinner. Besides tradition, an additional reason for having a fall season is that the turkeys are not breeding during this time, and hunting is less likely to impact the breeding time and affect the new turkey population.

Usually when a case is made against a fall turkey season, it's made by purist turkey hunters who believe young toms should not be harvested and that shooting a male bird less than a year old is not sporting. Some sportsmen prefer not to bag a gobbler unless his spurs are a certain length—perhaps one inch. Sometimes when hunters want to impose their own hunting codes on others, they petition their state departments of conservation to close the fall turkey season. The departments take these petitions, as well as the health of the turkey population, into consideration when making a decision about a fall season.

In the fall, a vertical camouflage pattern blends with tree trunks and naked branches.

## SETTING UP

In the fall woods, a turkey has a good chance of seeing you before he gets close enough for you to shoot. To conceal yourself properly, you have to rely on terrain breaks in addition to camo clothing and blinds. Putting a hill, a hump in the terrain, or a small ridge between you and the turkey will increase your odds of bagging that bird. That hump or hill will act as your blind. Then when the turkey walks into view, you can see him. If he's within gun range, you will have an opportunity to bag him.

Usually the best camouflage for fall is either predominantly gray or brown patterns. Since most of the leaves are gone by fall turkey season, tree-trunk patterns may prove to be the most appropriate.

I am convinced that turkeys can see a hunter much better in fall than they can in spring.

The floor of the forest is cleaner, and the hunter's silhouette stands out better. The fall turkey hunter must pay close attention to his camo and even may prefer to hunt with a blind. Because the woods are so open in the fall, where the hunter sets up is far more critical to his success than in the spring.

If you are forced to take a stand in an open area where a tom can see you 100 to 200 yards away, your chances for success are reduced. But never set up in a thicket or any kind of thick cover. Turkeys in the fall, like turkeys in the spring, avoid thickets. If you must set up in the open, sit still, and pray the turkey does not see you before he gets close enough for you to shoot.

One strategy some turkey hunters have used to bag fall gobblers is to hunt from treestands. Deer hunters know turkeys will walk under their stands and never look up to see them. This tactic

**If you find a flock of young gobblers feeding together, scatter them and listen for them to call. Then try to call them back.**

is especially effective if you know where turkeys are feeding every day. However, turkey hunting in the fall may mean covering a vast expanse of ground. Often when you locate a flock of turkeys, you will not have time to put up a tree-stand. But hunting from treestands can be effective if you scatter a flock of longbeards and plan to sit in one spot for some time.

## HUNTING YOUNG TURKEYS

Male turkeys, which are born in the spring, are called jakes in the fall. These birds are just learning to become gobblers. They have not had any hunter encounters, are not nearly as wary as their longbeard seniors, have not learned how to gobble, and have only two things on their minds—finding something to eat and staying with their mother and the other birds of their flock. The flocking instinct is very strong in both young gobblers and young hens, and the old hen's primary consideration is to keep her flock together and to warn them of danger. When fall turkey hunters find a flock of turkeys feeding together, they often scatter the flock to have a chance at the young gobblers.

Two words that sound similar but carry entirely different meanings when you are considering disrupting a flock are *scatter* and *scare*. When you *scatter* a flock of turkeys, you get as close as possible to the flock, and surprise them so the birds fly off in *different directions*. When you *scare* a flock of turkeys, you do not get close enough to them to create a scatter, but instead force most of the birds to run or fly off in the same direction. If you scare a flock of turkeys, you greatly reduce the likelihood of being able to call the birds back to you. When you scatter the flock, you do have a chance of calling the birds in and bagging a young tom.

When you see a flock of turkeys, do not immediately run at them and try to scatter them. Wait patiently, and determine in which direction the turkeys are feeding. Once you know the birds' line of travel, attempt to circle in front of them, take a stand, and wait for the birds to approach. Let the turkeys come to you.

Notice the makeup of the flock. Are any longbeards in the flock? Are the members primarily young hens and jakes? Or, have you lucked into a bachelor band of gobblers two years old or older? The age structure of the flock determines how to hunt the birds. If the flock contains mostly young birds—jakes and hens—then you know your hunt will be over quickly. If older gobblers are in the flock, your hunt may last until the end of the day or for the next three days.

If the flock consists of young turkeys let them come as close to you as possible, then jump up and run at the birds, yelling loudly. Run toward the center of the flock and scatter the birds in all directions. Notice in which direction most of the turkeys fly off.

Once the turkeys have taken to the air, find a stand site, preferably a large tree with a hill in front of you. Listen for the turkeys to call, which they'll do from five to thirty minutes after they have been scattered.

Two basic calls bring in young gobblers in the fall—the *kee-kee* run (the young gobbler's squealing call) and the old hen's assembly call. Young toms that have not yet learned to gobble make a high-pitched, *kee-kee* sound before giving a coarse yelp. These toms are trying to learn to talk. By giving the *kee-kee* run, you will sound like a lost jake calling other jakes to you. Because young gobblers want to regroup as soon as possible after they are scattered, this call brings them in.

The old hen assembly call consists of a series of loud, pleading yelps that start out slowly and then become louder and faster. This is the call made by the dominant hen to bring the flock together after it has been scattered. Often it brings young jakes to you on the run.

Often after you scatter a flock and begin to

call, a dominant hen may come in first and try to call the flock together. If she is successful, you may not get a shot. Your best tactic is to get up and run the old hen off. Then she will not have a chance to assemble the flock. After she has left the area, sit down, and begin to call again.

Young gobblers often come in quickly in groups of two or three as soon as you begin to call, so have your gun at the ready and be prepared to shoot. Wait until you can isolate one young tom from the group before you squeeze the trigger.

## HUNTING LONGBEARDS

The fall longbeard is the most difficult bird to bag, especially if he is a lone longbeard. A bachelor gobbler more than two years old that keeps to himself will test the mettle of any turkey hunter. In the fall, bachelor birds are very unpredictable, often antisocial and difficult to hunt.

Woodsmanship, more than any other factor, is the key to taking a fall longbeard. To hunt one, you have to know where he lives, where he feeds, where he roosts, and where he goes during the day. Generally you have to learn all this without hearing the bird talk. If the fall longbeard does make sounds, they will be very few. Patience is your strongest ally. Sit still for a long time and make very few calls. When the bird does come in, the only sound you hear may be his footsteps.

Your best chance for bagging a longbeard is to find a bachelor flock of two- and three-year-old birds, sometimes called amigos. This bachelor band may consist of three to thirty gobblers, depending on the local turkey population.

Turkeys are very social in nature. Often a bachelor flock remains together throughout much of the fall because they prefer one

**The longbeard of the fall is the toughest turkey to take, especially if he's a bachelor that keeps to himself. He's silent and extremely wary.**

another's company. However, the lure of running with the boys is in no way stronger than their will to survive. Regrouping after they have been scattered is not nearly as important to longbeards as it is to young gobblers. To bag a longbeard in a bachelor band, you must scatter the flock. Then, after the scatter, walk about fifty to a hundred yards in the direction you have seen several of the longbeards fly. Take a stand, and get comfortable. Wait thirty to forty-five minutes before giving one to three coarse gobbler yelps, which are much more drawn out and more raspy than a hen's yelp. Once you have made that call, wait forty-five minutes to an hour before you call again.

Longbeards are slow to regroup. Great patience and skill are required to call an amigo within gun range. Fifty percent of the time,

none of the amigos will return. These birds have survived for at least two years because they are woods-wise and hunter-shy.

Fall longbeards in a flock can be called. However, you may have to sit in the same spot and call for a half day or three consecutive days to get a shot. Generally if you are an experienced turkey hunter, have put in hours scouting and are a very confident caller, you should be able to bag a spring gobbler within three days. If you are an inexperienced hunter, plan on five days to two weeks to bag a fall gobbler.

Another tactic for fall hunting is to locate a flock of longbeards in the morning, scatter that flock and then hunt in another area until afternoon. About 2:00 or 3:00 p.m., return to the site where you have scattered the flocks, sit down, and then begin to call to the longbeards.

An amigo flock prefers the company of each other in the fall rather than consorting with a group of hens.

Patience is your greatest ally after you scatter a flock of longbeards like these and try to call them into range.

If the birds fail to come in by dark, leave the area, go home, get a good night's sleep, and return to that same spot at daylight the next morning with your lunch packed. Then you can sit and call all day long.

Boredom is your biggest enemy and patience your best ally when hunting the birds of fall. Determination most likely will prove to be your winning strategy.

If you take a fall amigo by calling, you deserve a trophy. You can pull your chair up to the table beside any of the nation's top turkey hunters. You have earned the right to be there.

## HUNTING THE "LONE WOLF"

The lone wolf of the fall is the ultimate prize. Even though his sex drive may cause his demise in the spring, in the fall he is the wisest, most elusive, most difficult to call, and the most highly prized creature in the woods.

A lone wolf may be the only gobbler that has survived from his entire year-class. In most areas of the country, a lone wolf will be at least four years old. In the fall, he shuns the company of not only hens and jakes but also amigos. He much prefers his own company to that

**Taking a longbeard in the fall is restricted to those hunters who live in one of the thirty-three states that have two turkey seasons.**

of any other bird, rarely is he social and usually he is moody. Because of his age, the lone wolf has learned just about every trick.

To bag a lone wolf gobbler, you must learn all you can about where he lives, roosts, feeds and travels before you ever attempt to call him. One of the best ways to obtain this information besides scouting may be by talking to deer hunters during deer season. Ask them if they spot a lone wolf in the woods to make mental notes about when and where he shows up and to share this information with you. Then you may have a chance to take him.

Once you pinpoint the lone wolf's home range, call very little, just enough to let the tom know another turkey is in his territory. Then the next move is the lone wolf's. When he decides he wants the company of another bird, he will come to your calling. If he does not want your company, he will not respond. Your most productive strategy is to play a waiting game.

More than likely when the lone wolf comes in, he will not announce his presence. He may spot you from fifty yards away, and you never will take him at that range. When a lone wolf does come in, he is keenly aware of danger and realizes he should see a hen. When he does not spot another turkey, he may leave the area.

A lone wolf may respond to gobbler yelps, hen calls or young gobbler squealing calls. Since this tom is an individual, no set rules can be laid down to bag him. Only by trial and error can you learn how to hunt him.

# 8

# Hunting the Eastern Wild Turkey

When the Pilgrims stepped off the Mayflower, they were just about out of food. They had eaten all the salted meat and dried vegetables they had packed for the trip and now wanted fresh meat cooked on an open fire.

When one of the first Pilgrims saw what he thought to be a huge chicken that was bigger and fatter than any of the chickens in his barnyard in England, he ran to catch it. But he found that not only could the chicken outrun him, it could fly too.

Ever since that day when the first colonists landed on the shores of the New World, Americans have been chasing those giant chickens we call turkeys.

The Indians had been hunting turkeys for years. They ate the meat and used the feathers for ceremonial robes, fletchings for arrows, and brooms to sweep out their lodges; the spurs for arrow points.

The eastern wild turkey, *Meleagris gallopavo silvestris*, which was the first wild turkey most Europeans encountered, soon became a staple food for the early frontiersmen. There were an estimated ten million eastern wild turkeys when the first settlers arrived, but during the 19th century, market hunters reduced their numbers drastically. Beginning in 1912, many states started restocking turkeys, and by 1989 the eastern turkey population was estimated at 3.5 million.

The eastern gobbler is distinguished from the Osceola, the Merriam and the Rio Grande mostly by color. The eastern is the darkest of all the turkey subspecies, ranging from chestnut to very dark brown. Their size varies according to region.

The eastern wild turkey is found from Florida to Maine and as far west as Iowa, and has the widest diversity of habitat of all the subspecies. Tactics for hunting these birds vary accordingly. Therefore, it is essential to understand the lay of the land through preseason scouting or from a study of topographic maps. Check the locations of streams, fences or other obstacles to avoid when setting up to call.

## MOUNTAIN TURKEYS

Mountain turkeys usually are much easier to locate than turkeys in flatlands and swamps. If you climb a high ridge and begin to call, you are apt to hear turkeys respond on both sides of the mountain and even farther away. At high altitudes, where there is less foliage, a turkey's gobbling travels far.

Another tactic for locating gobblers is to drive mountain roads, stop often and listen for turkeys on either side. Use an owl or a crow call to stimulate toms to gobble. Turkeys prefer to walk uphill rather than downhill, perhaps because when walking downhill most of their weight is forward of their legs. When you discover a tom in the mountains, the best places to set up are on the same level as the turkey or slightly higher. If the gobbler is on another mountain, perhaps on top of a ridge, climb to the top of that ridge and try to call the gobbler from there. Then he can walk straight toward you without going downhill. If the turkey is on the side of the ridge, take a calling position just above the bird and attempt to call him up to you.

Another problem with hunting mountain turkeys is the tendency to misjudge distance, especially if you are accustomed to hunting on flatlands in heavily foliaged forests. A bird gobbling from a tall tree on a high ridge may sound as though he is only a few yards away when actually he may be half a mile away.

Beware of echoes. If a gobbler is facing another mountain when he gobbles, the sound will bounce. If you are on the same side of the mountain as the turkey, he may sound as though he is on the opposite mountain.

During the spring, turkeys usually roost on mountaintops and either breed on a ridgetop or the valley. Usually turkeys feed in the valley unless there's an abundance of acorns or other foods on the ridges.

As the weather warms later in the spring, turkeys may feed in the valleys in the morning and move up where it's cooler in the middle of the day. Then they may come down when the temperature has cooled in the afternoon and fly to the ridgetops to roost at night. Most turkeys normally follow these general rules; however, certain birds always break the rules so assume that none of these rules are absolute.

My strategy for hunting mountain gobblers is either to walk the ridges or drive the roads between the mountains early in the morning to locate a gobbler. I hunt the bottoms of the mountains, the fields and the acorn flats after 9:00 a.m. In the middle of the day, I return to the ridges and remain there until I locate a turkey. I have learned you can locate more turkeys and reach them faster by calling from ridges.

## SWAMPLAND TOMS

When you hunt turkeys in swampy terrain, you have to accept the fact that you will probably have to cross water before the day is over.

Turkeys like to roost over water as a protection against predators. If they hear danger on one bank, they can fly to the other bank. So when you hunt swampland turkeys you can either wear hip waders, carry chest-high stocking foot waders and a pair of sneakers in a backpack, or get wet.

I usually carry a heavy-duty garbage bag and a roll of duct tape in the back of my hunting vest. If I have to swim a creek or wade water over armpit-deep to reach a turkey, I can put my boots, clothes and hunting vest in the garbage sack, tape the top shut and carry the sack and gun over my head when I slide into that cold spring water.

I spray all my clothing with insect repellent and carry a can with me to increase my protection against biting bugs whenever necessary.

Occasionally when you are hunting in a swamp, you will encounter a snake. But do not let your fear of snakes hinder you from hunting

**If you hunt in a swamp, assume you will get wet to bag your bird.**

turkeys in a swamp. Probably more turkey hunters who hunt in swamps are injured or killed in car accidents each year on the way to hunting than they are injured or killed by snakes. However, I am not foolhardy and look where I am going. Statistics indicate that snakebite is one of the rarest causes of death in the United States. Do not let fear inhibit you from hunting turkeys in a swamp just because snakes are there.

When you are hunting turkeys in thick swamp foliage, sound does not carry as far as in other terrain. A bird you barely can hear gobble may be only 150 yards or less away. If that same tom gobbles on top of a mountain, you probably would hear him half a mile or more away. If you hear a turkey gobbling loud in the swamps, you may be only thirty or forty yards from him. The best thing you can do is sit down quickly, call very little, and prepare to shoot.

**In the Deep South, most hunters search the swamps to bag the big longbeards.**

Swamp turkeys do not cover as much territory as mountain gobblers. Swamps usually have an abundance of food, and the birds do not have to go far to feed, roost, meet their hens, strut and drum. Often a swamp turkey roosts in the same tree for several nights. He may stay in that same general area—often less than 300 acres—throughout the entire day. Because the woods are often very thick in swamps, you rarely see the gobbler before he is within shooting distance.

## FIELD GOBBLERS

Turkeys that live on the edge of fields or around agricultural crops can be difficult to bag. Older, smarter birds have learned they can fly down into the middle of a field, feed, dust, strut, mate and see danger coming from all directions. I have met longbeards that flew from the roost to the middle of a field, remained there all day, and then flew up to their roost at dark. Some of these toms are almost impossible to take.

Generally turkeys roost in nearby woods, fly down into the woods, walk to the fields to feed, dust and mate, spend most of the morning there, move out of the fields as the sun gets hot and their dark feathers absorb that heat, loaf in the edge of the wood line in the shade until the temperature in the field begins to cool down in the afternoon, return to the field in the late afternoon to feed, dust and mate again, walk out of the field before dark back through the woods close to their roost and then fly up to their roost before dark. Although most field turkeys follow this schedule, some birds break these rules.

**Field gobblers are difficult to take because they have unobstructed views in all directions. This hunter managed to outwit a tom.**

Several tactics will help you take a field gobbler.

Set up at the edge of a field, and try to call the gobbler to that edge. This tactic is often effective when more than one gobbler is in a field. Most of the time, the dominant gobbler will stay with his harem of hens. But when a subordinate gobbler hears a hen calling just off the edge of a field, he may come running to you because he thinks he may have the opportunity to breed a hen before she goes to the older gobbler.

Challenge the dominant hen. A flock of hens and gobblers usually have a dominant hen that determines which way the flock feeds. If you consistently call to the gobbler with hen calls and that dominant hen thinks you are a rival for her position in the flock, she may come to the edge of the woods looking for you and bring the rest of the flock with her, including the old gobbler.

Wait until all the hens leave the gobbler in the middle of the field. When he is in the field and lonesome, you may be able to call him to you.

To locate field gobblers, drive roads through clearcuts and agricultural lands, and use binoculars or spotting scopes to look for gobblers. The best time of day to do this scouting is around 9:00 or 10:00 a.m., after most gobblers are off the roost and probably in the field.

Notice which way a gobbler enters and leaves a field. More than likely, he will take that same path each morning and afternoon. He has stuck to that route because he has never

A hunter gets to bag a gobbler that ventured away from his flock into a sparsely wooded area at the edge of a field.

encountered danger. Usually the route a gobbler takes to and from a field will be through open woods or big timber where he can see a great distance. If the turkey is walking to and from the field, you can take a stand along his route and call him to you. Often, very little calling is necessary to bag such a gobbler because you are sitting near the path he normally travels.

## BIG WOODS TURKEYS

The eastern wild turkey tends to like older timber and especially hardwoods. Hardwoods provide nuts the turkeys can feed on, shade where they can hide from the sun, and roosts where they can sleep at night. In many areas, turkeys spend most of their lives in big woods. When hunting open woodlots of mature timber, you can hear the turkeys gobble at a great distance.

Turkeys in the big woods are often found in the same areas as deer and squirrels because all three animals feed off the same forage. The more open the woods, the more likely you are to see turkeys. Because a turkey's number one defense is his eyesight, he prefers to stay in open places under the canopy of the forest where seeing you will be easy for him.

When I am hunting in big woods, I do more listening than I do walking. The turkey can hear you walking through the woods as you can hear him walking, which can be both an advantage and a disadvantage. If you walk like a hunter, the turkey probably will be spooked. However, if you walk like a turkey, the turkey's hearing you is an advantage.

When I'm walking through the woods, I try to make turkey noises. I try to sound like a hen walking through the woods as she goes through

**Eastern turkeys prefer to feed in hardwood forests in the company of squirrels and deer. All consume the same forage.**

her daily routine. Turkeys don't walk a regular, cadenced step as humans do. So I take erratic steps like a turkey—perhaps three steps and wait, then one step and wait again, then four steps, etc.

However, turkeys do make noise in a regular rhythm when they cluck, purr or scratch in the leaves. I try to imitate them. I scratch with my foot with a definite rhythm—scratch; scratch scratch; scratch. I try to cluck and purr in the same rhythm as feeding hens.

But remember, you are imitating the sounds of turkeys—the same sounds other hunters are expecting to hear. If you hear anything else walking in the woods, or any gobbler or hen sounds, stop where you are. Identify the sound and what's making it before you continue. If you see another hunter, give up the hunt, and use your natural voice to say in a very loud voice, "Hey, buddy, I'm not a turkey, I'm a hunter." When you walk like a turkey, you must be extremely careful to hunt defensively because the turkey you are fooling may be wearing camouflage instead of feathers.

## NORTHERN vs. SOUTHERN TURKEYS

The main difference between hunting northern and southern birds is their habitat. Generally the vast majority of turkeys in the North are hunted on public lands, in the South and the West, on private lands. Hunting tactics on public lands differ somewhat from those employed on private lands. When you hunt public lands and a turkey gobbles, you must get close to him and call him to you quickly before another hunter hears him gobble and beats you to it. Competition on public lands in the North is keen. However, if you don't take a tom in the first two hours after daylight, your chances of bagging one drastically increase after 9:30 a.m.

Turkey hunters often are two-hour hunters,

whether in the North, South or West. The highest concentration of hunters usually occurs an hour before to two hours after daybreak, and the birds soon adapt to this hunting pressure. If you are hunting turkeys in the North on public lands, from 9:00 a.m. on is the most productive time.

Some hunters believe that the eastern wild gobbler of the South is the toughest bird to take.

Ben Rodgers Lee of Coffeeville, Alabama, who was the grandfather of modern-day turkey hunting, once explained that, "Never have the wild turkeys in Alabama not been hunted in the spring. The turkeys that gobble the most get shot the quickest. The turkeys that gobble the least survive the longest. Through the pro-

**Terry Rohm, originally of Blain, Pennsylvania, out-hunted others on public lands by staying longer in the woods. He took this gobbler close to noon after other hunters had left.**

cess of natural selection, I believe Alabama hunters and those in other southern states one day will produce a turkey that will not gobble."

Southern turkey hunters tend to be more patient when calling gobblers. If an hour or two hours is required to call up a turkey, then the southern hunter will remain in his calling position and wait for a turkey to arrive. Because there are few hunters to compete with, the southern hunter will let a turkey gobble repeatedly and walk a long way to reach his stand. In the North, if a hunter waits an hour or two for a tom to come to him, more than likely someone else will bag that same bird. Southern hunters have a slower, more patient style of hunting than northerners, even though the birds are the same.

## MIDWESTERN GOBBLERS

Turkeys in the Midwest corn belt generally are larger and tend to gobble more than either southern or northern turkeys. Perhaps these birds have more food available and experience less hunting pressure. Missouri seems to be the mecca toward which all hunters of eastern wild turkeys bow. There, twenty-two pound gobblers are common, and hearing thirty to forty birds gobble in one morning is not unusual.

Because of the sheer numbers of turkeys available, the turkeys of the Midwest tend to be hunted differently than either the turkeys of the North or South. If you are hunting an eastern gobbler on either side of the Mason-Dixon Line, you may hunt that same gobbler all day long. But in the Midwest—especially in Missouri—you may have three or more toms to

**Brad Harris, of Neosho, Missouri, consistently takes large, midwestern gobblers weighing more than 20 pounds.**

work before your hunting day is over. Recently one morning in Missouri, Brad Harris and I called six gobblers to within gun range between daylight and 11:00 a.m. These turkeys seem to like much more calling than the birds in the East. A hunter can have a very good time calling often to these turkeys. In most instances, you will find more gobblers traveling together in the Midwest in the spring than you do in the North or South.

# 9

# Hunting the Osceola Turkey

Of the five races of wild turkey in the United States, the Osceola, or Florida, turkey is probably the most difficult bird to take. Not because the Osceola is more elusive than the others, but because its range is limited, finding places to hunt the bird is a problem.

The Osceola's home is in central and southern Florida where real estate is high and the demand for land is increasing. Most Osceolas are found on private ranches.

Two private hunting camps have Osceola populations that can be hunted for a fee. Fisheating Creek Hunting Camp in Palmdale has 20,000 acres in Glades County on Highway 27, on the western side of Lake Okeechobee, sixty miles south of Ft. Myers. Outdoor Adventures, a camp of 7,000 acres, is located near Orlando in Polk, Osceola, Lake and Sumter counties.

Besides private hunting camps, several Wildlife Mananagement Areas have good populations of Osceola turkeys. The 48,050-acre Green Swamp is one of the better public hunting areas in the state. It extends over Polk, Lake and Sumter counties about thirty miles north-

west of Lakeland. This area is protected and controlled and only can be entered through a checking station. Portions of this WMA have been control burned, and cattle are allowed to graze in this region, both practices helping to improve turkey habitat. Although Green Swamp WMA has a daily quota limit, you do not have to apply for a permit in advance.

Another WMA with turkey hunting is the 3,877-acre Andrews WMA in Levy County. Although this WMA is small, the turkey hunting can be good. However, because it is a quota WMA, a permit is necessary to hunt.

Upper Hillsboro WMA is another small region located in Sumter County northwest of Lakeland and consists of 5,178 acres with good Osceola turkey hunting on it. It normally is a primitive weapons only WMA, but during spring turkey season, shotguns are permitted on Wednesdays and Thursdays.

Other WMAs with good populations of Osceolas include the 28,000-acre Tosohatchee WMA and the 6,000-acre Seminole Ranch WMA, both in Orange County. However, the largest populations of Osceolas are found in

Osceola, Okeechobee and Glades counties.

The Osceola is nicknamed the swamp turkey after its natural habitat, but it has adapted to the Florida flatlands as well. Swamp turkeys are accustomed to water and will even wade when it is not above their knees.

The novice Osceola hunter quickly learns that another predator is competing with him—the bobcat. Florida has a large population of bobcats, and they can create problems for the hunter.

The Osceola turkey is intimately involved with the history of the Seminole nation. Named after the war chief of the Seminoles, this turkey has always been considered a bird of mystery owing to its uncanny ability seemingly to vanish into thin air.

Chief Osceola led his people into battle against one of America's finest generals, Andrew Jackson, handing Jackson his only defeat in the Indian wars of the early 1800s. Guerilla fighters who used hit-and-run tactics to defeat Jackson's army, Osceola and his men would appear and then disappear just as quickly. Many soldiers under Jackson attributed supernatural powers to the Chief, and the turkey that bears his name, *Meleagris gallopavo osceola*, is just as elusive.

When Allen Jenkins of the M.L. Lynch Call

**The Osceola gobbler is a bird of the palmettos and swamplands of Florida.**

The bobcat is the major predator of the Osceola and is responsible for keeping the turkey population under control. The Florida gobbler was named for Osceola, the famous Seminole war chief.

Company in Liberty, Mississippi, invited me to hunt these mystical gobblers with Marcelous Osceola, a direct descendant of the legendary chieftain, I was quick to seize the opportunity. This hunt was to be special. Jenkins and I were to teach Osceola how to call the wily Osceola gobbler, a technique known by his forefathers that Marcelous had never learned.

Today on the Big Cypress Swamp Indian Reservation near Miami, the Seminoles, like native Americans on most reservations, can take game throughout the year in any numbers for subsistence. Through the years, the harvesting of gobblers and hens for food primarily has been a rifle sport practiced around large fields and pastures on the reservation, a technique the Indians ironically have learned from the white man. But Osceola wanted to learn the tradi-

tional way of bagging the gobblers bearing his family's name.

When we arrived on the reservation late in the afternoon, we met friends of Jenkins who had been scouting and had heard and seen a few turkeys, but the gobblers had failed to respond to calling and had vanished. I unrolled my sleeping bag and donned 100 percent Deet repellent, which would be my shield during the entire trip from the clouds of mosquitos inundating the area at dark.

That evening, as we prepared our supper on a Coleman stove, Marcelous Osceola and his wife, Etau, came into camp. We talked about the upcoming hunt. Then Osceola explained the native religion of his people, a faith that attributed supernatural powers to the animal life of the swamp.

Etau Osceola with Florida gobbler. According to Seminole legend, the spirits of their ancestors are reincarnated in the wild turkey.

"If an owl flies through the camp during the annual festival of the Green Corn Dance, many believe the owl will capture someone's spirit, and they will die," Osceola told us. "Also, some of my people believe that the spirits of our ancestors are reincarnated in the wild turkeys."

When I asked Etau Osceola where this legend came from, she answered, "The wild turkey often appears and vanishes without ever making a sound. Sometimes we spot a turkey in a cemetery, and then it is gone in the blinking of an eye. The Osceola turkey is a ghostlike creature that moves silently through the swamp. You only hear him when he wants to be heard, and you only see him when he wants to be seen. When an Osceola gobbler spots you, he vanishes. The Osceola is a part of our people's history and heritage."

## THE HUNT FOR AN OSCEOLA

Before first light, the camp was up. Soon Jenkins, Osceola and I were out listening for gobblers. For a long time, the marsh was silent. Then, suddenly, a swamp gobbler began to crow. We climbed into our truck and drove toward the sound. But after forty-five minutes of calling, we could not find the tom.

In most areas of Florida, hunters scout for turkeys in cars. Much of the land is crisscrossed by roads. Wading through swamps or walking through the palmettos can be hazardous. You are attacked by biting insects, and you may meet a snake. The noise you make will probably spook the gobblers. Florida turkeys are not spooked by cars. They hear vehicles every day and are not afraid of them. Scouting in a car allows you to get closer to a turkey than you could on foot. Because of the dense foliage in many areas, you can drive within 150 to 200 yards of a gobbling bird.

"I can't believe I can't crank this gobbler up and make him talk," Jenkins said. "The bird has vanished, and I don't know where he's gone. Let's go see if we can locate another one."

We drove about two miles and listened. Once more we heard a turkey gobble. Again we drove toward the sound, but the gobbler was no longer there.

Because the Osceola turkey has a very limited range, and is subjected to a lot of hunting pressure, it is extremely wary and often call-shy, becoming silent and walking away from a call rather than responding to it.

"There's a pasture where I always see turkeys in the morning," Osceola mentioned. "Maybe we'll spot a gobbler there."

We drove about five miles, climbed out of Osceola's truck and walked down a raised dirt road between two pastures to reach a back pasture where Osceola had watched turkeys before. After we had walked about 150 yards, Jenkins suggested that we stop and listen for toms.

Within five minutes, a gobbler reported, apparently in the back field where Osceola had thought he would be. We moved quickly down the road to reach the corner of the field. Just as Jenkins, who was out in front, came to the edge of the back field, he motioned for Osceola and me to get down.

Part of the mystery and legend of the Osceola seems to stem from his habit of appearing and then vanishing in backwoods cemeteries.

The Osceola gobbler often leaves his swampy home early in the morning and ventures into the surrounding fields.

Crawling back to us, Jenkins whispered, "A longbeard is out in the field, but we don't have a place to hide. I'm going to set up my portable blind on the edge of the road. John, you can move off the edge of the road into the ditch and up beside the field and watch the turkey with your binoculars. Marcelous, you stay here behind the blind, and I'll try to call the turkey to you."

As I crawled to the ditch, I listened to Jenkins quietly telling Osceola how the hunt should go. There was no question that if the turkey came into range, Osceola would put the gobbler down. He had shot competitively on the trap and skeet circuit for some years and was a certified master with a shotgun. I crept through a small patch of briars to reach a vantage point from which to watch the drama unfold. I was confident of Jenkins's calling ability and Osce-

ola's skill. The only unknown factor in the equation was whether or not the turkey would be willing to come to the call. I peeked over the edge of the ditch and scanned the field with my binoculars, but I could not see the gobbler. The tom had quit talking, and the field was empty.

Jenkins is a patient hunter. He doesn't believe in hunting Florida turkeys aggressively. Because the birds are under so much hunting pressure, usually restrained calling and patient waiting are the best tactics. We waited for about ten minutes without hearing a sound. Then I spotted a huge, black dot in the very back of the field. As I watched through my binoculars I saw a bird that was smaller and darker than the eastern wild turkey. When Jenkins began to call, the gobbler seemed to key in to the sound like a beagle locked into the fresh scent of a rabbit. The turkey gobbled, walked a few steps and then strutted. Then he ran a few steps, stopped, strutted and gobbled. He was coming, and I had a ringside seat for the show.

Back in the blind, Osceola waited anxiously for the turkey to come within range. The gobbler continued to close ground rapidly while Jenkins sounded like the sexiest hen in the swamp. When the gobbler was twenty yards in front of Jenkins and Osceola, Jenkins clucked loudly. The tom stopped and craned his neck.

Boom! The sound echoed through the swamp, and the gobbler dropped in his tracks. When I arrived at a small wash, Jenkins was holding up a magnificent turkey and congratulating Osceola. Deep hues of burnt bronze and black reflected a green tint when the sun danced off the downed tom's feathers. With an eight-inch-long beard, this Florida gobbler was a fine trophy for Marcelous Osceola.

As Jenkins, Osceola and I headed back to camp, we discussed the future of the reservation's turkeys.

"Marcelous, if you and your friends want to have plenty of turkeys to hunt, don't take any

**Allen Jenkins, right, and Marcelous Osceola, with the big gobbler that bears his family name.**

**Big Osceola gobblers like this one can still be taken in a few areas of southern Florida.**

hens for a year or two," Jenkins counseled. "Don't shoot the young gobblers. Hunt only the longbeards. The reservation has plenty of food and habitat for turkeys. If you'll begin to protect the turkeys and take only longbeards in the spring, then in just a year or two, you'll have more gobblers to hunt than you've ever had. Every morning in the spring when you get up to go turkey hunting, you'll have a long-beard to call."

"That's what I want," Osceola said. "I'll learn to use this call and teach my brother how to call. Then we'll start hunting the way you guys do. Calling and hunting with a shotgun is a much more interesting way to take turkeys than shooting them at 100 yards with a high-powered rifle."

That night at camp, Osceola treated us to a Seminole feast. We ate fried alligator tail from an animal he had taken the day before. The meat was delicious, and the conversation around the campfire was even better. We talked about the ways of the Seminoles, their past, present and future. We discussed the Osceola turkey and its future on the reservation. Even though I hadn't taken a turkey, the hunt was a success. It was enough to hunt the gobblers of the Florida Everglades with a descendant of the man they were named for. That's a memory I'll treasure as long as I live.

# 10

# Bagging Rio Grandes

Half asleep in the saddle, the cowboy listens to the light mooing of the herd that has been bedded down all night. His old Winchester 94 30/30 rifle fits snugly in its saddle scabbard, and the leather of his saddle squeaks slightly as his buckskin mare walks among the longhorns.

Then off in the distance, the familiar sound of cows wailing to the moon triggers a new sound just before daylight. From the cottonwoods near the creek, he hears the gobbles of Rio Grande turkeys. On this day, the cowboy will feast on a turkey dinner.

Just before first light, the leather-chapped rider steers his steed toward the cottonwoods. Walking in the shallow creek bottom, he notices a turkey tail fanned on the edge of the rimrock. As the horse turns to go up a small wash, he pulls his Winchester from its scabbard. A coyote howls, and the turkey gobbles.

Seventy yards away, three fine gobblers strut on the plains with their harem of hens. The rider brings his Winchester to his shoulder; his cheek finds the cool, hard wood of the stock. He cocks the hammer, looks down the iron, and pulls the trigger. The turkey tumbles.

The plainsmen of the old West rarely used shotguns. A rifle that could be carried on their saddle could take almost any game. With a rifle, they could defend their herds from rustlers and predators, and harvest the game they needed for food. The early frontiersmen saw little need for any weapons other than a pistol and a rifle. As in most areas of the country, tradition dies hard. Today, hunters in the West generally use rifles.

The turkeys in the West never had been considered as much of a prize. Western hunters were beef eaters, with an occasional deer, antelope and jack rabbit thrown in when times were tough. Although turkeys were plentiful, they were rarely in high demand. Yard chickens provided the Sunday meal.

The Rio Grande turkeys, found primarily in Texas, at times numbered around 500,000 birds. These Texas turkeys were not subjected to as much hunting pressure as eastern turkeys. Their primary enemies were coyotes, foxes and bobcats. Today, with the decrease in the predator population and the protection offered these birds, their numbers have exploded.

The Rio Grande turkey, living as it does in the arid southwestern deserts, seeks the shade of trees whenever possible.

A couple of years ago, I had the opportunity to hunt on lands in Wheeler County, Texas, where the turkeys had never been called to or hunted with a shotgun. These virgin Rio Grande gobblers liked to hear calling and would come to you quicker than you could get your gun up. The two birds I took were four-year-olds that sported 1½-inch spurs and weighed 22 pounds each.

The next year when I hunted in Sonora, Texas, I could hear thirty or forty turkeys gobble in the morning and saw plenty of turkeys all day. However, it took me two days to bag a trophy bird.

The Rio Grande gobbler presents a different challenge than either the Osceola or the eastern wild turkey. Because trees are so scarce in the desert, finding one hundred birds in a small group of cottonwoods is not uncommon. Since the land is so flat and dry, the sound of a turkey's gobbling often can be heard almost a mile away.

Generally the Rio Grande likes to hear more calling than the eastern turkey or the Osceola. Most Rios I have hunted must be called incessantly to keep their attention and bring them in. More than likely, if you are hunting where the Rio population is large, you will call in three or four gobblers at one time.

Usually, when the Rio Grande gobbler flies from his roost, he is going to feed. In desert areas, he normally follows the same trail every

The author with a fine Rio taken near an old stock tank.

day. Like deer trails, these trails are often well defined. If you set up a calling position in the morning near one of these trails, you will doubtless call in a tom.

After he has fed and the sun begins to heat up the desert floor, the Rio Grande gobbler searches for shade. If you do not take him immediately after he flies down from the roost or on his way to a feeding site, there are two other places you can catch up to this bird. From 10:00 a.m. until late in the afternoon, he will be looking for shade and water. If you take a stand near a stock tank in the middle of the day, often you will see a longbeard.

The main problem with hunting Rios is the lack of cover. Allen Jenkins, one of my favorite hunting companions, and I once chased Rios all morning before finding a stock tank in a pasture at 11:00 a.m. When we called, several turkeys gobbled. There were no big trees or bushes nearby where we could take cover, but we spotted an abandoned, rusty calf feeder between the stock tank and the turkeys. Jenkins and I climbed inside. As we called, a flock of fifty turkeys containing six longbeards started moving toward us. We shot one of them.

If you are fortunate enough to hunt Rio Grande turkeys, often the landowner can tell you where he has seen some. However, most Texas ranchers are not turkey hunters. If you are on a piece of property and do not know where to hunt, look for water. Most of the time when you locate a stream running through the land you are hunting, you will encounter Rios. The turkeys need drinking water; their food, as well as their roosting trees, grows near water.

**Allen Jenkins, left, and John Phillips with a Rio Grande gobbler taken near an abandoned calf feeder.**

These trees and bushes also provide shade the turkey needs to dodge the hot desert sun. And the streambeds also provide cover for hunters.

## HUNTING TACTICS

One of the mistakes made by most hunters who hunt Rio Grande gobblers for the first time is shooting the first big birds they see. Because of the large number of gobblers they often find concentrated in one place, they tend to take the easy tom. However, because Rio Grande turkeys are not pressured nearly as hard as eastern gobblers, if they were patient, they'd possibly harvest a trophy Rio.

When you hear Rios gobble in the morning, move in close to the roost site, and begin to call. The turkeys usually gobble as they fly from the roost to their feeding area. Often this feeding region won't be near your stand. You have to chase the gobblers and catch up to them. If you can get ahead of the birds, you may be able to call them to you. If you cannot, accept the first day of your hunt as a learning exercise. Notice in which direction the turkeys fly from the roost; more than likely they'll fly in the same direction the next morning. Find the trails to their feeding areas. Learn the shady places they frequent after they feed. Look for water holes, streams and creeks, and notice the trails the birds use to return to their roost sites. If you take a day to scout the Rios in the area, you will be more successful on the second day of your hunt.

A few years ago, I hunted with Cecil Carder on the 4-M Ranch near Sonora, Texas. Although we had several opportunities to take turkeys on the second day of the hunt, fate always seemed to deal the birds the winning hand.

This Rio sought shade from the hot desert sun under a large tree, only to encounter a bow-hunter who was waiting for him.

Then late in the afternoon, about two hours before fly-up time, we spotted a big gobbler on the edge of a field with a harem of fifteen hens. Since a dry river bed skirted the field, Carder and I got into the river bed and sneaked around behind the turkeys. As we neared the spot where the tom strutted with his hens, we saw a natural dirt ramp cutting through the bank of the hill that went down to the river and up the other bank. This ramp looked like a natural place where a turkey could walk from the bank across the river bed and up the other bank. Carder and I decided to take a stand in a small plum thicket on the edge of the ramp. Although calling a longbeard gobbler away from his hens would be difficult at best, we knew this chance would be the only one we would have to bag this big bird this day.

Because the gobbler had so many hens with him, we did not call as aggressively as we normally would but chose instead to call a little and wait a lot. Each time we called, the gobbler answered aggressively. However, as the sun went down, the turkey still had not come to us. Finally in the last rays of light, just before fly-up time, the hens filtered through the plum thicket. The Mossy Oak camouflage Carder

Rio Grandes need plenty of water in their hot and arid habitat. One of the best places to take a stand is near a stream or pond.

**Preston Pittman hangs my big Rio Grande gobbler in a tree on the edge of a creek to foil coyotes. Then we continued to find another turkey.**

and I were wearing prevented the females from seeing us as the hens walked within six feet of where we sat motionless.

I saw the ivory-colored head of a royal Rio moving toward the ramp. The bird was in full strut and about thirty yards from where I was sitting. In the low light, I looked through the scope on my three-inch magnum and immediately spotted the gobbler's head. When the turkey was directly in front of me in full strut, Carder clucked one time on a pushbutton call. When he did, the big bird dropped his strut and craned his neck to see what had caused a hen to cluck.   At that moment, my crosshairs found the bird's wattles, and I squeezed the trigger. Although the Rio was a huge tom, his beard was only 2½ inches long. I wondered if I had shot the beard off since this gobbler was fully mature, with 1½-inch spurs. When Carder saw the bird and looked at the beard, he began to laugh. He said, "Congratulations, John, you've just bagged the world's-record jake."

I was convinced the turkey had to be at least three or four years old and was not a jake. After Carder stopped laughing, he explained that sometimes Rios get mites in their beards that eat on these hairlike protrusions. Apparently this turkey had had a case of mites that had eaten up most of his beard. We both laughed, put the big bird on my shoulders, and headed back to camp.

**Cecil Carder with a Rio we took on the edge of a creek late in the afternoon.**

To hunt Rios, you must be in good physical condition. A hunter must cover more ground to locate and call turkeys in Texas than he does in the East. You may have to walk five miles in the morning looking for a Rio. These toms often travel three or four miles before returning to their roost.

Binoculars are important for hunting Rios in Texas. You can spot a turkey at much greater range in Texas than in the more wooded East. You need to know whether the bird is a gobbler or a hen before you begin the hunt.

Camouflage is another important piece of equipment. Brown camouflage is helpful cover for the desert areas. Compared to the East the western turkey's terrain is rather bleak. Sneaking and crawling behind bushes and ground cover, as practiced in the East, will not work.

Because there is so little cover in Rio country, most novice hunters think that using a blind makes sense. But if the wind causes your blind to move or flap, you will spook more turkeys than you take. If you do use a portable blind, the best place to set it up is on the downwind side of a big tree (if you can find one). Or lean brush and limbs against the blind to protect it from the wind and give it a more natural appearance.

In most areas of Texas, baiting is permitted for turkeys. The obvious place to take a stand is close to a feeder. Then you can bag the birds as they come in to feed. However, many animals will come to the feeder besides the turkeys—including javelinas, deer and coyotes—and often will spook the turkeys.

A better tactic is to take a stand along a trail the Rios use to go to and from the feeder. Probably the turkeys have learned that a feeder not only represents food but also danger from predators, and they usually approach cautiously. If you take a stand 100 to 150 yards away from the feeder, the birds are not likely to spot you.

Sitting close to a feeder and killing a turkey is not my idea of turkey hunting. I enjoy calling the bird, convincing him that I'm the sexiest hen on the desert, and getting the bird so excited he performs an unnatural act like coming to a hen rather than making the hen come to him. When you sit beside a feeder and shoot a bird that is coming to feed on corn, you are not a turkey hunter; you are a turkey shooter.

The Rio Grande gobbler is the turkey of the West. To complete your hunting experience, make a trip to the country of the longhorn and match wits with this desert rascal.

# 11

# Hunting Merriams

The Merriam wild turkey is found in the deserts and mountains of the West. In the desert areas just about everything that grows contains thorns, and you need to carry a pad or cushion to sit on for protection. If you hunt the mountain Merriams, and you are a flatlander, you must suck in four mouthfuls of air to equal one mouthful of air at sea level.

If you are a flatlander prepare for a Merriam hunt by climbing stadium steps daily for at least six to eight weeks and plan to arrive a day or two early at your destination to allow your body to adjust to the altitude. Despite these drawbacks, I enjoy hunting Merriams and have learned many lessons from them. Besides, Merriams are beautiful and majestic birds, and just observing them is a treat in itself.

Merriam turkeys inhabit a wide range, from Minnesota to California, including Nebraska, South Dakota, Colorado, New Mexico and Washington. In much of this range, the birds are found high in the mountains. I learned that the best way to find and take Merriams is to stay on the mountaintops and call to the birds below. To bag a Merriam, get above him. If the turkey is

gobbling on the side of a mountain, you may not have to climb to the top to reach a calling position, just high enough to take a stand above him.

Wind is often the enemy of the Merriam hunter. On a hunt on the Smith Ranch in New Mexico, I learned how wind can affect hunting. This property was very dry, with turkeys primarily found in or near canyons. For three days, the wind blew so hard we rarely heard a tom gobble. All we could do was remain on the floor of a canyon and wait for the wind to die down. After an hour-and-a-half wait on the third day, the wind finally ceased.

As soon as a calm fell over the canyon, we heard a turkey gobbling from the cottonwoods along the edge of a creek. We got down in the creek, walked under the lip of the bank, and took a calling position about 100 yards from the bird. The turkey immediately answered our calls and started coming toward us. When the gobbler was thirty-two steps from us, I squeezed the trigger of my Remington 3-inch magnum SP—and the bird tumbled. As if some unseen hand was at work, as soon as the shot was fired and the gobbler fell, the wind

Hunting mountain Merriams requires hard climbing. Be sure you're in top condition before going after this bird.

Best strategy for hunting mountain Merriams is to climb above them before starting to call.

The author waited three days for the wind to die down so he could hear a turkey gobble. Then he bagged this Merriam from a stand in a creek bed.

A hunter calls to a Merriam in the mountains. In this type of terrain, you can cover more ground with less effort on horseback.

started to blow again—almost blowing the feathers off the downed bird. In three days of hunting, we had only that one hour-and-a-half break from the wind, but that was long enough to hear and call my Merriam.

Because hunting Merriams can be so physically grueling, many westerners travel on horseback. It is my favorite way to go after the mountain gobblers. Mountain-trained horses can climb steep, rocky paths and descend into deep gorges without stumbling. If you have to cross three mountains to reach a bird, you can go faster and easier on a horse than you can on foot. Because the horse is a natural part of the environment usually it won't spook a gobbler nearly as quickly as a man on foot will. Another advantage to riding a horse is that when you reach an area where

you want to call, you can tie up the horse or hobble it and move in close to the birds. Then if the gobbler comes in quickly, you will not be breathing hard, your muscles will not quiver from exhaustion and you can hold your shotgun steady. Also, if you take a bird, you can tie him to your saddlehorn by his feet and carry him out of the woods effortlessly.

Most hunters use a blind when hunting Merriams in open and arid terrain. However, the intense wind may move the blind and that may spook a turkey. A blind may not be the best solution to the lack of cover in Merriam territory. Camouflage clothing is your best bet for concealing yourself from gobblers, both in the East and the West.

Because the air in the West is usually thin

High winds in Merriam country may make a blind impractical. Camo clothing to match the terrain is your best bet.

Because sound bounces off canyon walls, a hunter may think a gobbler is on one side of a canyon when actually he is on the other.

and clear, sound travels farther than it does in the East, often bouncing off canyons and echoing through the mountains. Thus the whereabouts of a gobbling Merriam is usually difficult to determine. That's why I listen to a Merriam turkey gobble for a long time and have a pretty good idea where he is before I decide to chase him. When you hunt Merriams, wait longer, listen more, and if possible, have a friend listen twenty to thirty yards away.

## EQUIPMENT FOR HUNTING MERRIAMS

You need good pair of binoculars or a spotting scope to hunt in the vast country of the West. Spotting scopes and binoculars are especially effective when the wind is high and hearing

Author with a big Merriam tom taken in New Mexico. Pile of bleached antlers and skulls testifies that this is also deer country.

turkeys gobble is difficult. On a windy day, you probably will see more turkeys than you hear. It is much easier to get lost in the mountains of the West than in the East. The West does not have as many fences, roads, fields and firebreaks as the East. In the home range of the Merriams, you may walk all day and never see a sign left by another human. Therefore, you should always carry a compass and learn how to use it properly. Take standard survival equipment with you, including waterproof matches, a space blanket, extra food, some lightweight rope or strong string, medicine, and anything else that will make an overnight stay in the outdoors comfortable. The fear of getting lost is much like the fear of having an auto accident. If you realize it can happen, you will exercise extra caution.

# 12

## Bagging Turkeys
## With Blackpowder Shotguns

I was caught as unprepared as a baby on his first birthday. The turkey had gobbled less than thirty yards away. We stood in the middle of the road, with no place to run and no place to hide. We dropped to our knees.

"Can you see him, John?" Bo Pitman whispered.

"No, there's a little hump in the road in front of me. I can't see him, but I can hear him," I answered quietly.

By now the gobbler was screaming, and the leaves on the trees quivered from the force of his gobble. Pitman nocked an arrow, and I nocked the hammer of my blackpowder shotgun. We had planned this to be a primitive-weapon hunt. We had agreed that Pitman would take the first shot. If he could not make the shot, or if he missed, I would back him up with my smoke pole.

"I can't draw, John," Pitman said in a low voice. "You'll have to take the shot. The bird's at twenty yards. Go ahead and shoot him."

"I still can't see the bird because of the rise in the hill," I said. "Is the gobbler to the left or right of my gun barrel?"

"He's straight in front of you," Pitman said. "He's less than eighteen yards. Please take the shot."

I still couldn't see the bird. "He's in full strut, John," Pitman reported. "Take the shot."

The tom was so close I could hear him spit when he drummed. Finally, just over the top of the hill, I spotted the gobbler's white crown. My cheek was on the stock, the hammer was back, and the bead on my blackpowder shotgun was superimposed over the wattles on the gobbler's neck. Because the turkey knew he should be seeing the hen at this range, he became very nervous. He putted, made two quick steps forward and stopped. His neck went up like a periscope, and I let the hammer fall. When I fired, gray smoke filled the air in front of my face. Pitman was up and running before I could gain my feet and reached the

**Bo Pitman and the black-powder shotgun he uses to hunt gobblers.**

bird before I did. We discovered there had been no need to hurry; the blackpowder shotgun had performed for me as well as it had for the early frontiersmen.

## GUNS AND LOADS

Most blackpowder shotguns today are cylinder bore, which means they are straight pieces of pipe that are not choked or narrowed down to tighten the pattern. For this reason, the pattern will spread, and taking a turkey at more than twenty yards is difficult.

However, there is a blackpowder shotgun on the market that is fitted with screw-in chokes: Connecticut Valley Arm's (CVA) Trapper shot-

gun. You can have a full-choke barrel by simply screwing one of these new choking systems into the Trapper, which was designed by CVA for the growing sport of hunting turkeys with black powder. Not only does this single-shot blackpowder shotgun have a screw-in choking system, it also has posts for a sling and a recoil pad.

Although CVA and other manufacturers do produce double-barrel blackpowder shotguns, most of these are also cylinder bore. Even though you gain another shot with a double barrel, you still lose the tightness of the pattern.

I prefer the CVA Trapper for hunting turkeys. When I aim at the wattles on a turkey head target, seventeen shots will be in the turkey's head and neck area at thirty yards with a full choke screw-in tube. Without the tube,

The author took this fine specimen with his blackpowder shotgun.

Pyrodex does. However, blackpowder hunters often argue about this theory. On clear, dry days, often Pyrodex is preferred because it tends to burn cleaner.

By testing both powder charges, you can determine which charge produces the best pattern for you. I find that the 1⅛-ounce charge usually yields a denser pattern. Often when I test the 1¼-ounce charge, the additional powder tends to blow the pattern out, spreading the shot over a wider area. The shot does not stay as dense in the target area as it does when I use the 1⅛-ounce charge. However, each gun shoots somewhat differently, and the combination of wadding and shot may have various effects with each of these two charges.

Another method of improving your pattern without adding or reducing your powder charge is to change the amount or type of overpowder wadding or cushion you use. If you

only one to three shots will be in this same target at this distance.

When you hunt with black powder, you have an advantage over the conventional shotgun hunter because you can modify each individual load. You can improve the pattern of your shotgun in several ways.

You can use more or less powder. Most blackpowder shotguns can handle 1⅛ to 1¼ ounces of powder. One and one-eighth ounces of Pyrodex is equal to 80 grains of 2F black powder. The 1¼-ounce charge of Pyrodex is equal to 90 grains of 2F black powder. You can use either Pyrodex or black powder when formulating your charges.

The choice of powder also can be changed according to weather conditions. Generally, 2F black powder is preferred on rainy or humid days. This old conventional black powder does not seem to absorb as much moisture as

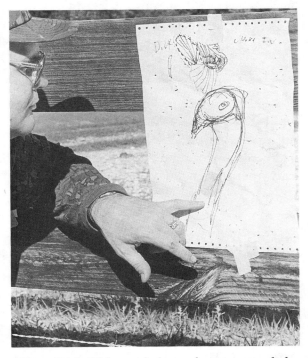

When Dick Kirby and the author patterned the CVA Trapper shotgun with a turkey head target, they found it put seventeen pellets in the kill zone.

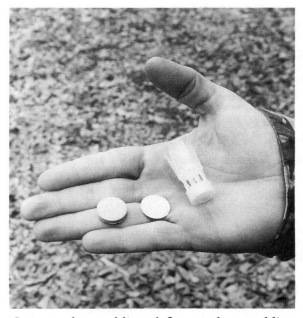

**Overpowder wadding, left, overshot wadding and plastic shot cup can be changed to improve your pattern.**

select a cardboard kind of overpowder wadding, you often can change your pattern by trimming the thickness of the cardboard to increase or decrease the size of the wadding.

Yet another way to tighten your pattern is to use plastic shot cups like those found in modern-day shotgun shells. I prefer this type of wadding because I believe less deformity occurs in the shot when the powder is ignited and the shot travels down the barrel than with cardboard type of wadding. The modern plastic shot cup seems to have a better cushion in it to absorb some of the shock when the powder explodes. This shock-absorbing feature of the plastic shot cup prevents the lead pellets from being excessively smashed together and deformed when the powder explodes. Once the shot leaves the barrel, the plastic shot cup seems to hold the shot together longer, which I think tends to produce a tighter pattern. On the other hand, many blackpowder hunters believe cardboard wadding shoots just as tight a

pattern as a plastic shot cup. Use the wadding system that produces the best pattern for you and your gun. Regardless of which type of wadding system you prefer, you must use an overshot cardboard patch to keep the shot from rolling out the end of the barrel.

Another option that determines pattern density is the amount of pressure you use to pack your load. Many blackpowder shotgunners are convinced the overpowder wadding and the overshot wadding must be rammed home and forced down the barrel snugly. However, if you pack the powder and the shot tightly in the barrel by adding more pressure to the ramrod, you can decrease the volume of the powder and increase the rate at which it expands. If you ram your shot and cup home too hard, you may compress the powder so tightly that you blow out your shot pattern.

I particularly enjoy blackpowder hunting with a shotgun for turkey or any other game because I can customize my loads with powder, patches and shot until I get the type of shot pattern I want for that day of hunting. I have determined that my best load is 1⅛ ounces of powder, a plastic shot cup, 1⅛ ounces by volume of No. 6 shot and a cardboard overshot patch.

I have experimented with duplex loads mixing No. 4 and 6 shot, and even combining No. 2, 4 and 6 shot. However, I have found that for the gun I shoot, the No. 6 shot produces the densest pattern at thirty yards. Remember, each gun patterns differently. You may discover that No. 4s or 7½s will produce a better shot pattern in your gun. The more pellets you can put in a turkey head target at thirty yards, the better your odds for bagging a bird with a blackpowder shotgun.

## BLACKPOWDER ACCESSORIES

I have found a few accessories essential for hunting turkeys with a blackpowder shotgun.

**Sling.** I prefer to have a sling on my shotgun. Just because you are carrying a blackpowder gun does not mean your hunt for a gobbler will be any different. Since often you have to cover long distances in a day, a sling can make carrying a gun more comfortable.

**Nipple Protector and Cap Guard.** I like to use a hard plastic nipple protector, which allows me to carry my gun at half-cock with the cap on the nipple without the danger of the gun going off. When I use a nipple protector, I also can cock my gun when I sit down to call a gobbler. I leave the nipple protector on the nipple until the turkey is close and then simply slide the protector off the nipple to be ready to fire. This system eliminates having to cock the hammer and perhaps spooking the turkey.

A cap guard is a small plastic ring which secures the cap to the nipple.

**Muzzle Protector.** A muzzle protector will prevent moisture from getting in the barrel. A rubber finger, available at drugstores, works very well.

**Recoil Pad.** A recoil pad on the butt of the shotgun protects your shoulder from the strong recoil of this weapon.

**Fiberglass Ramrod.** This is a useful tool for the blackpowder hunter. Wooden ramrods often break, but fiberglass is very durable.

**Cleaning Jag and Patch Puller.** Carry an extra cleaning jag and a patch puller in case your regular jag gets stuck in the barrel. Without these two accessories, your hunt may be spoiled.

**Speedloaders.** These are handy for carrying additional powder charges and shot into the field. The speedloader lets you pre-measure your shot and powder and put them in small cylinders that you can carry in your shirt pocket with several overshot patches and the same number of shot cups. This system reduces the amount of equipment you have to carry in

Cap guard (left) secures the cap to the nipple, preventing it from falling off and causing a misfire. Nipple protector (right) keeps the gun from firing, even when the hammer is down. It also keeps your powder dry.

Shot goes in one end of speedloader, powder in the other. It fits in a pocket.

Possibles tool combines many blackpowder tools into one neat knifelike device.

the field if you need to reload while hunting.

**Possibles Tool.** One problem when hunting turkeys with black powder is being weighed down by too mich equipment. A CVA possibles tool contains several gadgets in one compact knifelike accessory.

## TRICKS OF THE TRADE

One of the worst things that can happen to a turkey hunter shooting a blackpowder shotgun is to call a turkey into range, squeeze the trigger, and have his gun misfire. I have found a method to reduce the chances of a misfire. Before I go out in the morning, after I have loaded my gun I remove the nipple and pour a few grains of powder down the nipple hole. Then I take my nipple pick and clean the nip-

Dick Kirby, president of Quaker Boy Calls, with a trophy gobbler taken with black powder.

Hunting turkeys with a blackpowder shotgun is the ultimate challenge, and taking a long-spurred gobbler is one of the rewards.

ple one more time to make sure I have a clear channel for the fire from the cap to go down the nipple and ignite the powder. Next I place a cap guard over the cap, which secures it to the nipple. With this system I have almost eliminated the problem of misfires.

When I am calling up a turkey I plan to take with a conventional shotgun, I usually think my maximum effective range, even with a 3-inch magnum 12-gauge, is 35 yards. However, most of the time I will not shoot unless the bird is at 30 yards or less. I generally apply this same extra 5-yard rule when hunting turkeys with black powder.

Although I have bagged birds with a blackpowder gun at 12 yards, I do not advise letting the tom get that close. Your shot pattern will not spread sufficiently at that close range.

Hunting gobblers with a blackpowder shotgun is not that much different from hunting with a conventional shotgun. The primary differences are:

• You must formulate your own shot.
• There are more chances that something can go wrong.
• You usually have to let the bird get closer than you do with a conventional shotgun.
• You have to cock the hammer without spooking the turkey.
• You have to "keep your powder dry."

Two of the fastest growing sports in America today are turkey hunting and blackpowder hunting. Blackpowder hunting is a logical progression in your evolution as a turkey hunter. A turkey hunter must first learn to hunt turkeys with a conventional shotgun and have some success bagging birds before he moves on to black powder. Blackpowder hunting adds a new dimension to the sport and tests the hunter's skills to an even greater extent.

# 13

## Bowhunting for Turkeys

Bowhunting for turkeys is not a beginner's sport. Primarily two kinds of people take up their bows to pursue longbeards—bowmen who have shot tournament archery or who have been successful bagging deer, and hunters who have taken numbers of turkeys with a shotgun and who want to bag a gobbler the old way. A problem with bowhunting turkeys is the bird's small vital area, which is protected by a profusion of feathers and meat. A tom turkey presents an illusion. Although he appears to be a large target, underneath all those feathers he has a small body. A turkey's head is too small a target and moves too quickly for the bowhunter to have a reasonable chance of placing an arrow there. More about this later in the chapter.

Most turkey hunters agree you must call up ten times as many gobblers to get a shot with a bow as you do with a gun. Bowhunting for turkeys requires you to do most of the things you are not supposed to do when you hunt turkeys. For instance, normally when a turkey is less than thirty yards away, you must not move because the bird will see you. But when you are bowhunting for gobblers, you must draw your bow when the tom is that close. When you are bowhunting other game, the quicker you draw, aim and shoot, usually the more effective your shot will be. However, when you are bowhunting for turkeys, you usually have to hold the bow at full draw for some time before releasing the arrow. The strain may cause muscle fatigue, and you are likely to miss.

### EQUIPMENT

Although plenty of equipment has been designed specifically for taking turkeys with a bow, most archers I know who consistently harvest toms every spring use almost the same equipment they use for deer. Because the target on a turkey is so small, accuracy is vital, and you'll feel more comfortable with familiar equipment. However, since turkeys are more sensitive to sound, it is advisable to modify your bow.

"I take my bow apart, separate the limbs from the risers and put pool table felt between

Holding a bow at full draw while waiting for a clear shot at a turkey puts great stress on an archer's muscles.

the risers and the limbs to quiet my bow for turkey season," says Ronnie Strickland master bow-hunter of Natchez, Mississippi.

Strickland also uses large puffs on his string to quiet the bow even more. He places felt on his arrow rests and waxes his arrows with furniture polish to keep them from making sounds as they pass across the felt.

"One of the best ways to find out just how noisy your bow is, is to go into a closed room and draw," Strickland suggests. "Probably you'll be surprised at how much noise it makes. If you can hear the bow being drawn, the turkey can too."

Some hunters believe that a heavy bow which drives an arrow at high speed increases the chances of hitting a turkey before he moves. On the other hand, as noted previously, if you have to hold a heavy bow at full draw for some time, you are likely to miss the bird. Many

Most hunters modify their bow for turkey hunting to make it as silent as possible. Ronnie Strickland, shown here at full draw, attaches puffs to his bowstring to muffle the sound.

turkey hunters believe that a 50- to 60-pound bow is more than adequate for downing a longbeard.

Comfort is the best test for choosing a bow. If you have been shooting a 50-pound bow all year and can hold this bow at full draw for a long time, then probably you should not change the poundage to hunt turkeys. If you have been shooting a 70-pound bow in field archery and during deer season, and you feel comfortable holding a 70-pound bow at full draw for an extended time, then a 70-pounder may be the best bow for you.

## Broadheads

In choosing a broadhead for turkeys, consider the shocking power. Turkeys are very quick. If an arrow zips through them, more than likely they will fly or run a long way before they expire. For that reason most bowhunters favor big broadheads with the ability to disable a gobbler quickly.

"I like the 180-grain Simmons Interceptor with an arrow stopper behind it," says Ronnie Strickland. "The bigger broadhead will do more damage quicker than the smaller broadhead will, and the arrow stopper will keep the

**A typical broadhead (top) often used for hunting deer but favored by many for turkeys. Below, the new Turkey Spur from Wasp which stops the flight of the arrow and holds the broadhead in the bird.**

arrow in the bird and help to prevent him from running off. I believe that shocking power and arrow placement are the keys to recovering the turkey when you are bowhunting."

Wasp Archery Products has developed the Wasp Turkey Spur, a six-blade Cam-Lok broadhead, specifically for turkey hunting with bows. Three of its interchangeable blades have been enhanced with spurlike claws to impede penetration and provide shocking power. The spurs prevent escape by not allowing the broad-head to exit the animal. The three remaining blades are replaceable, razor-sharp, vented carbon blades, fine-tuned for precision flight.

## String Trackers

Adding a string tracker to your bow and arrow can increase the odds of your finding a gobbler

after he has been hit. However, if you plan to use a string tracker, practice with this device before you go into the field. The closer a turkey is to the bowman, the more effective a string tracker is. At longer ranges, the string tracker will inhibit arrow flight. Once again you must make a decision as to whether you want to shoot more accurately or use a device that will aid in recovering your bird.

Before you bowhunt, find out if a tracking dog is in the area where you plan to hunt. A bird dog, or a dog that has been trained to trail and locate turkeys, will improve your chances of finding a tom once he has been shot.

## Blinds

I have hunted turkeys with and without the aid of a blind. Both methods work.

**String trackers help you locate a bird after he's shot, but they may inhibit the flight of the arrow at long ranges.**

Without back cover, this bowhunter risks being seen when he draws by his sharp-eyed quarry.

A blind that completely covers the hunter allows him to draw without fear of detection. Decoy distracts the turkey's attention.

In many areas, being able to move quickly and efficiently to get into a better position to take a shot at a turkey is critical to your success. Some bowhunters believe you can move and set up faster without a blind. Of course, then a turkey has a better chance of spotting you.

"Often when bowhunters set up, they don't think about back cover," Ronnie Strickland explains. "If you're silhouetted without back cover, the gobbler is more likely to see you when you draw. I also like to have plenty of cover on either side of me. Then the tom can't watch me draw, and I can wait on the bird to step in front of me. Side cover often is just as critical as back cover when you're hunting without a blind."

In many areas of the East, finding this much cover is not too difficult. But locating turkeys in sufficient number to increase your odds for taking one with a bow can be very difficult. However, when you are hunting Rio Grandes in the West, you may hear lots of birds but lack sufficient cover to hide your movement.

According to Strickland, "Having a blind is more critical to your success in the West than in the East."

John Demp Grace of York, Alabama, both a master archer and a fine turkey hunter, has wrestled with the problem of bagging eastern birds with a bow for many years. Finally, Grace has developed a blind that totally covers the hunter but has several shooting ports on all sides. The blind is quickly and easily assembled and provides cover on all sides and above. For some years now, Grace has harvested his limit of six turkeys per season with a bow using this type of blind.

Because blinds have a distinctive shape, and the wind can blow the material around, most hunters break up the silhouette with brush, which also keeps the material from moving in the wind.

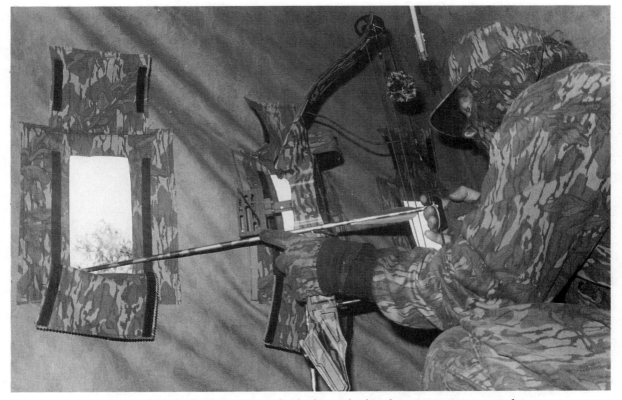

Inside a blind, the hunter can look through the shooting ports, spot the turkey and draw when he is ready.

## Decoys

No one ever has made a foolproof aid that always attracts a gobbler. Remember this when you use a turkey decoy. A turkey decoy may cause a gobbler to approach or to stay away.

If a gobbler sees a decoy he believes to be a hen, he knows instinctively that all he has to do is strut and drum to attract her. The tom probably will stop fifty or sixty yards away from the hen, perform his mating ritual, and demand she come to him. If she does not respond, he may walk away from her. But a gobbler may be so fired-up about mating that when he sees the hen, he will come trotting to her and attempt to mate.

A decoy diverts the attention of the gobbler from the hunter. Then you may have time to draw your bow without the turkey's seeing you.

When the turkey comes in, he will be looking at the decoy rather than searching for you or your blind.

Most bowhunters generally agree that a decoy is a decided advantage in states where it is permitted. Be sure to check your local regulations.

## Camouflage Clothing and Boots

As with all other forms of turkey hunting, you should wear full camo from head to toe. Where you anchor the bowstring before the shot often determines the type of hat, gloves and face camo you wear.

Hunters who anchor on the tip of the nose, in the corner of the mouth, or on the side of the face generally feel a headnet inhibits their ability to anchor correctly or may get caught in

This bowhunter has turned the bill of his cap to the rear to keep it from getting in the way when he draws .

the string when they release. For this reason, many archers use camouflage paint for their faces instead of headnets. The bill of the cap also can interfere with the archer's ability to make the shot. Some hunters wear their hats backwards, with the bill off to the side, or choose a short-billed cap designed just for bowhunting.

Hand camo is also a concern of bowhunters who use fingers, tabs or a release system. Often a bowhunter chooses camo paint instead of gloves to give him a better feel for the bow and string. Once again, the camo you choose should be the camo with which you are most comfortable. If you bowhunt for deer with camo gloves and a camo facenet, and you can draw smoothly and shoot comfortably wearing these two items, then

there is no reason to change your camo system for turkey season.

## CALLING

One of the most effective ways to take a turkey with a bow is for one hunter to call while the other takes the shot. Using this system, two hunters can take advantage of their individual expertise. Generally the caller takes a stand twenty to thirty yards behind the bowman and tries to call the turkey into range. The caller can concentrate all his efforts into putting the turkey in front of the bowman, while the latter focuses on getting into position and taking the shot.

If you plan to hunt turkeys alone, then you

With the proper camouflage, a hunter almost vanishes in the woods.
Then he has to guard against moving and making noise.

must learn to use a diaphragm call, which frees your hands for bow handling. Often you need to make just one more cluck to bring a turkey a step or two closer while you hold the bow at full draw. The diaphragm allows you to do this.

## WHEN TO DRAW AND SHOOT

If you are hunting from a blind, you can draw and shoot whenever the turkey is in range. But if you are not concealed in a blind, you should draw only when the turkey cannot see you. The situation becomes especially complicated when more than one turkey comes to your call. Attempting to hide from one pair of keen eyes is difficult; when two or three pairs are looking for you, drawing unseen can be almost impossible if you are not in a blind.

If only one turkey is in front of you when you are ready to draw, wait for the turkey to step behind a tree or a bush before you draw. If there is no tree or bush in the turkey's path, or if the bird is in full strut, wait for him to turn away from you with his tail fanned. When a turkey fans his tail and lays his head back in his feathers during his strut, he cannot see behind him. Then you can draw undetected.

The worst-case scenario for hunting gobblers with a bow is if a turkey does not step behind a tree and does not strut. Then your best chance to draw is when the tom lowers his head to feed. But even then, more than likely the bird will see you.

## SHOT PLACEMENT

Most bowmen who hunt wild turkeys agree the most critical skill is shot placement. Where the

A bowman draws on a turkey called in by his partner. Working as a team is one of the most effective ways to hunt turkeys.

**When a turkey turns his back to you shoot for the base of the fan.**

arrow enters the turkey's body determines whether you will be able to find the bird once it falls. Usually a hit along the backbone will stop the turkey and is the best place to aim.

The turkey's spine can be reached from several different routes. If a bird is facing a shooting port of your blind head-on, aim for the place where the beard comes out of the feathers. If the tom gives you a side view, point your arrow at the spot where the wing butt attaches to the body. If the gobbler is standing with his fanned tail to your shooting port, aim for the anus or the upper center of the fan, slightly above the anus. Here is a look at where master bow hunters aim at gobblers with their bows.

David Hale of Cadiz, Kentucky, one of the owners of Knight & Hale Game Calls and a leading turkey hunter with either gun or bow, prefers to shoot at the turkey's back. "Since the spine shot in my opinion is the best shot you can make on a turkey, if a bird is going away from me or has his back to me, then I take the opportunity to shoot for the spine. If the gobbler is in the strut, I'll shoot for the spot where the wings join the body—again hoping to get a spine shot. If you shoot into the turkey's breast, more than likely you'll lose the bird. If the turkey has his tail fanned in a strut with his back to me, I shoot for the spot where the tail feathers join the body."

Dale Faust prefers the spine shot to avoid having to search for a wounded bird.

Once you have taken a turkey with a bow, you have moved into an elite class of hunters.

Dale Faust of Centreville, Mississippi, who has won 3-D silhouette shoots, field archery competition, and numerous other awards, agrees with Hale that, "The best shot to take at a turkey is the spine shot. Because turkeys don't leave a blood trail like deer and other big-game animals, you may have a difficult time retrieving the bird otherwise."

However, when Faust is aiming at a turkey that is quartering away from him, he does not shoot for where the wings enter the body, as most hunters do. Instead, he directs his arrow just above the spot where the drumsticks join the tom's body because, "This vital area is where you most effectively can get a quick kill.

Many times if you're shooting down on a gobbler and you hit the point of the wings, the arrow will go through the breast rather than through the vitals. That's why I use the drumsticks of a bird to point the way to the region I sight in on and then hit."

Brad Harris, public relations director for Lohman's Manufacturing in Neosho, Missouri, has been hunting turkeys with a bow for more than fifteen years. Harris is convinced that shot placement is the most critical part of the hunt.

"If you put the broadhead into the turkey where it should go, you won't need a string tracker or any type of arrow-stopping device."

# 14

## Hunting Safely

Each year some hunters are shot while turkey hunting. It is a sport in which the hunter imitates the game, and may be mistaken for his quarry by another hunter.

But just how safe is turkey hunting? Is the sport more dangerous than deer hunting? To find the answer, I talked with Gene Smith, editor of *Turkey Call* magazine and director of publications for the National Wild Turkey Federation (NWTF).

"Turkey hunting is much safer than it often is perceived," Smith reports. "About 75 percent of the accidents that occur while turkey hunting are the result of the hunter being mistaken for game. However, when you consider accidents per 100,000, which is the way accidents are judged, far fewer happen while turkey hunting than in many other sports."

In the latest report on turkey hunting accidents, the Erickson Report, twenty-eight states were surveyed. The survey showed that of the more than 10 million man-days spent in the woods, there were 198 accidental shootings. *Accident Facts*, a national publication of the National Safety Council, reports that in a typical year, the number of deaths per 100,000 for parachuting is 72.5, 41.3 for hang gliding, 4.5 for scuba diving, 2.5 for boating, and 2.5 for swimming.

Nevertheless, you have to take certain precautions in the turkey woods. Do not be so intent on bagging a tom that you forget to be a safe hunter. No turkey—not even a world's-record tom—is worth becoming a hunting statistic or causing someone else to become one.

## TEN RULES FOR SAFE TURKEY HUNTING

1) Never stalk a turkey. If a turkey is gobbling in front of you, do not to sneak up on him and shoot him. A gobbling bird calls in hunters. If another hunter has sat down, started to call to that tom and hears you walking in the area, you may be mistaken for game.

The sound of a man walking is similar to the sound made by a walking gobbler. A man crawling on his hands and knees is about the same height as a turkey. If another hunter is in

Do not crawl when stalking a turkey. You will appear to be the same height as a gobbler for which other hunters are also searching.

Do not wear a white tee-shirt under your camouflage clothing or you may be mistaken for the white-crowned head of a gobbler.

dim light and looking for a turkey, he may mistake you for one. If you plan to ambush a turkey rather than call to him, learn the direction the bird is going and set up far enough in front of him so you won't be mistaken for him. If you want to call to the bird, sit down. Never attempt to sneak up on a gobbling turkey.

2) Do not wear the colors of the flag—red, white and blue. The colors of a turkey's head are red, white and blue. He has blue cheeks, red wattles and a white crown. A turkey hunter searches for these three colors. If you wear these colors, the chances of your being mistaken for a turkey are greatly increased. Other common mistakes include:

• Wearing a white tee-shirt under your camouflage outfit. If your mask or camouflage gapes open and reveals just some of that white tee-

shirt, another hunter may mistake you for game.

• Wearing a red bandana, a red or white handkerchief, or any other red clothing. Do not wear a red shirt on cool mornings under your camo shirt.

• Carrying white toilet paper into the woods to be used when nature calls. The movement of that white toilet paper can cause a hunting accident. Some companies make camouflaged toilet paper, which is an absolute must for the turkey hunter. I check out my hunting partner before I go into the woods. If I see any red, blue or white on him, I caution him about what may happen. I ask my partner to look me over to see if he can spot any of the three danger colors on me.

3) Do not continue calling when you see another hunter. If another hunter is approach-

ing your stand, do not wave to him or try to divert him from your position by using your hands. Remember, that hunter is looking for movement. If you see another hunter coming toward you and you are sitting on the ground, remain perfectly still. Allow him to walk by if he is in the distance.

If the hunter is close, speak to him in your normal voice and tell him, "Hey, buddy, I'm over here." If he answers you, say, "I'm to your left, and I'm about to stand up. Don't shoot." When some hunters see another hunter approaching, they continue to call, hoping they can call a gobbling turkey to them before the other hunter has a chance to get to the turkey. However, if you keep on calling, even if you are using a mouth diaphragm, you will move slightly, the hunter will know exactly where you are, and he may assume you are a turkey.

Even if you are making hen calls, the other hunter may think a gobbler is with that hen and may stalk you. Never call when you spot another hunter. Also never move until you have identified yourself with your natural voice, and the other hunter has answered you.

4) Never try to get closer than 100 yards to a turkey on the roost. If the turkey is gobbling from the roost, most hunters set up about 100 yards from the bird and expect the bird to be coming to them within that 100-yard range. If you move in closer than 100 yards and walk around, then you are inside the range where a hunter expects a turkey to be walking. Another hunter may assume that what he has seen and heard is a gobbler that has flown down from the roost and is walking toward him. Never walk toward a roost tree after fly-down time. Always assume another turkey hunter is set up

**Do not carry a red or white handkerchief or use white toilet paper in the turkey woods. They may be mistaken for a gobbler's head.**

on that same bird. Consider the area within 100 yards of a roost tree no man's land. If you decide to go there, travel with extreme caution, and expect another hunter to be in the region.

5) Never use a gobbler call unless you are in a defensive position. When you make the call of a wild turkey gobbler, you are producing the sounds the turkey hunter is hunting. You entice hunters to hunt you. If you decide to use a gobbler call, make sure you have your back against a tree much wider than your shoulders. Be certain you can see in all directions and that no hunter can slip up on you. When you decide to leave the spot from which you have been calling, before you stand up, give an owl call, a crow call or a hawk call, or bark like a dog, or use your natural voice to let someone know where you are. Always make sounds other than turkey sounds to let someone who may have come in behind you know you are not a turkey.

Using a gobbler call on public lands is one of the most dangerous sins a turkey hunter can commit. I advise using a gobbler call only when you hunt on private lands.

6) Select open calling sites. When you take a stand to call a turkey, do not be so well-hidden you cannot see all around you. Do not take a stand in bushes that may be shaken if you move your gun barrel or reposition yourself. If your blind prevents your seeing in all directions, another hunter may slip in near you without your seeing him.

7) Protect your back. The gunfighters of the Old West always sat with their back to the wall. Then no one could slip in behind them undetected. Remember this defensive position when turkey hunting. If your back is protected by a large tree, a bank, or some other type of barrier, then if another hunter does approach, you should be able to see him. If another hunter shoots at a turkey that walks up behind you, you are protected.

8) Camouflage does not make you invisible. In most of today's camouflage advertisements,

One of the reasons for taking a stand in front of a large tree is to protect your back from another hunter who may shoot at a turkey behind you.

manufacturers use words like "invisible," "vanish," "blend in" and "disappear" to make you believe a turkey won't see you. Often this gives the hunter a false sense of security. You may think that if you remain motionless you will not be seen. However, when you move, another hunter may not be able to identify you. A turkey hunter is looking for movement.

9) Do not shoot at sound or movement. Being the cause of a hunting accident is as bad as being the victim. One of the reasons an experienced turkey hunter may be involved in a hunting accident is because he feels he must shoot a turkey.

In a turkey hunting camp the night before a

hunt, a sportsman with a reputation may have to endure some ribbing from his buddies "Hey Joe, how come you haven't gotten a gobbler this season? You usually have bagged one or two by now. What's the matter? Are you losing your touch?"

When one hunter puts that kind of pressure on another hunter, the teaser is cocking the hammer on a loaded gun. Then the other hunter thinks he has his reputation to uphold and that to regain his stature in camp, he must return to camp with a bird. If he sees something that looks or moves like a turkey, he may shoot much quicker than usual.

Instead, talk in your hunting camp about the number of hunters in the woods. Emphasize to all that each must be careful when hunting turkeys.

10) Assume every sound is a hunter. Paul Butski of Niagara Falls, New York, hunts public lands in his home state and always practices defensive hunting. When I hunted with Butski, he explained, "John, when hunting public lands, always think every call and sound is made by a hunter. Assume each piece of red, white and blue you see is a hunter's clothing, and don't fire a shot until the bird proves to you he's not a hunter.

"Look for a tom's beard first. Next try to see his wattles. Search for his eyes. Then see one feather clearly before taking a shot. When I'm hunting public lands, I always assume I'm calling another hunter. I make the turkey prove he's not a hunter before I shoot." Butski's philosophy is defensive turkey hunting. If we practice this, we will eliminate accidents.

Hunting private lands may give you a sense of false security. When you and your buddy are

To practice defensive hunting, always make a turkey prove that he is not a hunter before you shoot.

the only two hunters on private land, you may assume you cannot run into each other in the woods. However, if either of you starts moving on a gobbler and repositions yourself, you may walk into each other's territory. Or, a hunter may accidentally walk off his land and onto your land. A poacher may be sneaking through your woods. Do not be trapped into believing that just because no other hunters are suppose to be in the woods that you can shoot any sound or movement you think is a turkey.

Once a friend of mine and his son were hunting private land and had separated to hunt two different turkeys. Later in the morning, the man, who was an experienced turkey hunter with many seasons to his credit, spotted what he thought was a gobbler. He raised his gun, fired and shot his son. Accidents can happen. But if you hunt defensively, never shoot at movement or sound and always clearly identify a turkey before you squeeze the trigger, you can prevent accidents.

A turkey decoy can attract a gobbler, but it can also deceive another hunter.

## OTHER SAFETY TIPS

Many states now permit hunters to use a decoy when calling in a turkey. These lifelike replicas of both hens and gobblers move in the wind and resemble a live bird. When a hunter spots a decoy, has heard what sounds like a turkey, sees something move that resembles a turkey, he may fire.

When you use a turkey decoy, do not take a stand immediately behind the decoy but on either side. Then if an unsuspecting hunter does see and shoot your decoy, you will not be in the line of fire.

Although it is rare for a hunter to mistake a dead gobbler for a live one, the best way to carry a turkey out of the woods is to place him in a hunter-orange vest or put a hunter orange flag on the vest once you are through hunting. Never leave a turkey's head hanging out of your game bag. If possible, put the tail feathers inside the bag, also. By hiding anything that looks like a turkey, you are more likely to prevent accidents from occurring.

Although the chances of being bitten by a snake while turkey hunting are remote, you should still take precautions. Do not be foolish. Since snakes often lie beside logs, before you step over a log, look carefully. If possible, step on the log, look down, and then step over it. If you are wading the edge of a creek or a stream, keep your eye out for a snake.

Always carry insect repellent with you. No matter how much repellent I have put on before I hunt, before I start moving toward a gobbling bird or sit down to call, I spray my entire body with insect repellent.

Insect repellent will keep mosquitoes, ticks and redbugs from attacking you while you are calling

Never leave the turkey's head hanging out of your vest (left). Another hunter may spot that head and mistake it for a live gobbler. Wear a hunter-orange flag on the back of your vest (right) when you are carrying out a turkey.

Snakes are also a hazard in some parts of the country, although accidents are rare. Always check the other side of a log before you step over it.

a turkey. Mosquitoes buzzing around your eyes and ears and lighting on your gloves, can distract you and interfere with your aim. Also, if you have to swat at mosquitoes or scratch insect bites, you will be making movements that may resemble a turkey to another hunter.

The number one accident that befalls hunters is getting lost in the woods. The gobble of the bronze baron has such a hypnotic effect you may be so intent on bagging the bird that you may lose your way in the woods. Even hunters who carry compasses still get lost in turkey woods. Always take a small emergency blanket to keep you warm if you do have to spend the night in the woods. Carry waterproof matches, a few candy bars, a knife and other items to make your night's stay comfortable.

Remember, no one plans to get lost, but if you do become lost, wait to get found. Once you realize you are lost, do not panic. Build a fire, and wait for someone to find you. A fire not only provides light at night but also is a signal to would-be rescuers. If you decide to walk out, follow drainages until you find a bridge or some type of crossing, or walk ridgetops where you can see a long way. Always tell someone where you will be hunting, and when you will be back. Then if you are late, someone can look for you.

# 15

# Caring for Your Bird

The gobbler stands twenty yards away. Your shotgun is resting on your knee, your cheek is on the stock; you have just pushed the safety off, and the bead on the gun comes to rest on the turkey's wattles as your fingers slowly and gently begin to caress the trigger. The gun explodes and carries its swarm of pellets to the target. What happens next determines whether or not you will have a fine gobbler to eat or mount.

When a turkey is hit, very rarely will he fall motionless. Often a turkey will flop and begin to bounce around on the ground. Even though the bird is dead, his body does not know that yet. The tom may begin to beat the ground with his wings and his body, which will knock beautiful feathers off him and create bald spots which may or may not be repairable by a taxidermist.

After you have fired, get up quickly and hurry to the turkey. Grab the bird by his feet and lift him off the ground, allowing him to beat the air with his wings. This prevents the turkey from bouncing around on the ground and knocking off many of his feathers.

If you plan to eat the bird, you need to field-dress him. Begin by cutting a small hole around the anal area. Reach inside the turkey. Pull out all the entrails, being sure to remove all the red, spongy lung material, which can spoil very quickly. Do not wash the inside of the carcass since water will increase bacteria build-up. After you have removed the entrails, the bird is ready to be carried out of the woods.

Decide now whether you will pluck or skin the bird to prepare it for cooking. If you choose to skin the gobbler, do it in the woods when you are field-dressing him. With either method, you still can save the prized parts of the bird, such as the tail, the spurs and the feet, for mounting.

The classic method of carrying a turkey is to throw him over your shoulder, holding him by the feet. But after you have walked 100 yards, you will realize that those round, bony legs supporting 16-pounds-plus of turkey will severely cramp your shoulder and weaken your muscles. If you have some type of strap, tie a noose around the turkey's head and feet and carry the turkey on your shoulder by the strap. If for some reason you do not have on hand a turkey toter or a turkey vest, use the sling on

If you are going to cook the turkey, field-dress him immediately after he's down and pluck him when you arrive home.

your shotgun to carry out the bird. The best method is to put the turkey in a turkey vest, being careful to fold his wings and not damage his tail feathers.

If the bird is to be mounted, do not remove the entrails. Take care when folding the wings and protect the tail feathers if you are carrying the gobbler in a vest. If any feathers are loose on the ground—especially wing feathers or tail feathers—be sure to pick them up and carry them with you.

When you get the turkey to the car, be conscious of the temperature. If you are hunting in the spring, when the temperature reaches 60 or 70 degrees, and you put the bird in the trunk of your car, the inside of the trunk will be even hotter and spoil your trophy. Instead, put the turkey on the floorboard of the back seat, and leave the

windows down so the air can circulate.

The best method to get a turkey home from the field is to take a 100-quart cooler with you. Whenever I hunt or fish, I always carry a 100-quart cooler in my car. With a cooler this size, I can take cold drinks and food and have plenty of storage space for my bird. I also keep on hand 30-gallon trash bags. Then I can put the turkey inside a trash bag, pull the drawstrings tight around his legs, and place the bird in the cooler. The bird will stay cool and dry with little or no chance of spoiling, even if I am in the field for a day or two.

If you plan on mounting the bird, the sooner you can get him to a taxidermist, the better your chances are of having a quality mount. If you want to eat the bird, the quicker you can get him plucked and on ice, in a refrigerator

**If you want to mount your bird, don't remove the entrails in the woods. Put him in your game bag, carefully folding the wings and protecting the tail feathers, and carry him home in a cooler.**

and/or in a freezer, the better the meat will be. Whether you plan to eat a turkey or mount him, never leave the gobbler in the trunk of your car and drive all over town for a day or two showing him to your friends.

## PREPARING YOUR GOBBLER FOR COOKING OR FREEZING

After field-dressing the gobbler before you leave the woods, pluck him as soon as you arrive home. If the bird is still warm, the feathers will probably come out quite easily. But if the bird has cooled, a wet plucking is preferable.

The simplest way to pluck a turkey is to dunk it into steaming hot water. Allow it to soak a minute or two. Slosh it around to make sure it gets completely wet. Remove it from the water. Then begin to pluck it in the same direction the feathers grow—from the neck toward the feet. Do not pull the feathers backwards, which may tear the skin. Next, singe your turkey to make sure you have removed all the pinfeathers. A pair of tweezers may be needed to do this properly.

You also can skin a turkey, a chore you can complete before you leave the woods. The breast and the legs, which are the main edible parts of a wild turkey, take up minimal space in a cooler. Some hunters, especially those who intend to be in camp for a day or two before returning home, debone each side of the breast to allow the turkey to cool quicker, thereby also conserving their cooler space.

To skin a turkey, tie one or both feet to a limb, and use your fingers to tear the feathered skin away from the flesh. The cut made in the anal area where you removed the entrails is a good place to begin the skinning process. Drop unwanted parts of the bird into a trash bag to keep the woods clean. Use another trash bag for parts you may wish to save for mounting—the tail, the wings, the lower legs, and the beard.

The turkey's skin is tender when the bird is freshly dead and will come away in large tears. Once the skin and feathers are removed, use a knife to cut the breast away from the back, and cut off the wings at the joint. Cut off the legs as well. (In some areas, you may be required to leave a tag on the leg of your gobbler until you reach home. Some regulations also may require the beard to stay on the carcass of a spring turkey.)

If you plan on cooking the turkey in one or two days, then store the bird in the refrigerator. However, be sure to cover the bird, and put it in the meat cooler if possible. If it is to be frozen for cooking later, triple wrap the parts of the bird using clear plastic, then foil, then freezer paper, packing each layer very tightly to eliminate any air and any chances of freezer burn. On the outside of the package, write the turkey's weight and the date it was put into the freezer. A turkey tastes best if cooked within two months of the kill, but it can last as long as one year in the freezer.

## CARING FOR THE TROPHY

Besides writing, I also operate a part-time taxidermy business. I will never forget the day a proud hunter brought in a 22-pound eastern gobbler that sported an 11-inch beard and 1¼-inch spurs.

"I want to get the bird mounted because he's the biggest bird I've ever taken," the customer told me. "But I don't know where I'm going to hang him once he's mounted. My wife's an artist. She says we're not having any dead bird

hung in our house. I either have to put him in my office or in my basement, but he's too fine a bird not to mount."

I agreed with the hunter. When he left, I began to mount the bird. The mounting and drying process took several months. When the turkey finally was completed, he was mounted flying and was a fine-looking bird. I called the man's home to notify him his turkey was ready. But he was out of town. His wife agreed to pick up the turkey. I heard some reluctance in her voice at having to perform a task she was not eager to do. However, when the woman arrived at my shop, her attitude changed.

"That's the most gorgeous bird I've ever seen," she exclaimed. "I never realized a turkey's feathers contain so many iridescent colors. Look at how the bird seems to change colors when you change its position or the lighting. I can't believe something as ugly as a turkey can be so beautiful and that this is what a wild turkey looks like. I'll surprise my husband. He'll be gone for two weeks."

I helped the lady load the turkey into her van and was excited that someone else had discovered the rare beauty of the wild turkey. After a couple of days, I had forgotten about the artist and the gobbler. Three weeks later, my telephone rang. On the other end of the line was the hunter whose wife had picked up his turkey.

He told me, "John, you're not going to believe what happened. When I came in from a business trip, I walked into my living room and in the center of the wall where my wife's favorite painting once hung was my gobbler. The bird almost seemed to glow. When I looked up at the ceiling, I realized my wife had called in an electrician and had special lighting put in to hit the bird from different directions and cause his iridescent feathers to shine. The turkey seemed to change colors as I moved around him. As I stood there looking at my turkey, my wife came in and said, 'Isn't he beautiful, honey?' "

## DECIDING ON A MOUNT

If you plan to mount your turkey, you do not want to trust your prized possession to just anyone who claims to be a taxidermist. The best way to select a taxidermist is to look at an example of his work. Actually, the best time to make this choice is prior to turkey hunting season when you have plenty of time to look around. Remember, allow your taxidermist time to do a good job. Taxidermy is an art.

### Mounting The Head

Before you arrive at the taxidermist's with your gobbler, you must decide how you want the turkey's head, the most colorful part of the mount, to be prepared. Through the years, I have observed the evolution of techniques for mounting a wild turkey's head. The first taxidermists' only option was to skin the head and neck, remove the meat, preserve the wattles and skin as best they could, and pray that the skin would not crack for at least two or three years.

Later, polyurethane and latex rubber heads, which could be easily and unnoticeably attached to the turkey's body, became available to taxidermists. However, many of these heads looked artificial, although they were not subject to cracking.

Another method, which I consider the best,

**Plenty of wall space is required to mount a turkey in flying position. Be sure to measure your wall before deciding on this pose.**

now is available for preserving the turkey's head—freeze-drying. In this process, the gobbler's neck and head are removed, posed in a lifelike position and placed in a freeze-dry machine, which removes all the moisture without shrinkage. The process keeps the head intact, preserves it, and eliminates cracking.

The number one complaint of hunters about their turkey mounts usually is the color of the gobbler's head. Seldom can a gobbler's head be restored to the same exact color it was when the turkey was bagged. The turkey's head must be painted to restore the color that is lost once a tom is killed. To insure your turkey's head is the color you want, understand clearly what your taxidermist intends to do.

### Your Turkey's Pose

Other factors to consider are where the mount will be displayed and what the turkey's posture will be. Where the mount will be displayed will dictate the pose of your gobbler. If the room where you will hang your mounted trophy is small, a turkey in flying position may not be a good choice. Rather, a walking, sneaking or strutting mount may be better. To decide which pose you prefer, measure the area where the mount will stand or hang. Check these measurements with your taxidermist to be certain your trophy and mounting position will suit the place you have chosen.

## COOKING YOUR TURKEY

In these days of eating healthy for our hearts, most all of us are aware of the merits of eating turkey, a meat low in cholesterol and fat but packed with protein. Today's grocery stores feature turkey steaks, ground turkey and turkey sausage, as well as turkey breasts and whole turkeys.

Unlike domestic turkeys, the wild turkey is not bred for its breast meat. This lack of breast meat may disappoint most first-timers. The meat is also drier than a domestic turkey's, due to the wild bird's lack of fat. If you roast the turkey, baste it generously to keep the meat moist and flavorful. A cheesecloth placed over the breast and kept moist with a buttery sauce is a good method. The recipe you select will determine the kind of basting sauce you use. One of my favorites consists of a ½ cup of orange juice, ½ cup of butter, and a small amount of grated orange peel for added flavor.

It's advisable to remove the legs from the turkey and cook them separately. Often the breast will dry out while the legs are still cooking if they are cooked together. I often cook the legs and wings separately from the breast, sometimes using a different recipe.

To prepare your turkey for cooking, dry pick and singe it, and wash with warm water (4 teaspoons soda to the gallon). Remove the tendons. Soak the fowl in salt water (4 tablespoons salt to a gallon of water) for 3 to 3½ hours. Pour off the salt water, wash the turkey, and rub well with lemon juice. Then proceed with any roasting or baking recipe.

### Oven Fried Turkey

8 cups packaged herb-seasoned stuffing mix
12- to 16-pound turkey, cut up
salt
pepper
¾ cup butter or margarine, melted

Crush stuffing finely. Sprinkle turkey pieces with salt and pepper. Brush with melted butter or margarine; roll in stuffing crumbs. Place pieces skin side up without crowding in greased shallow baking pan. Drizzle with any remaining butter or margarine. Cover pan with foil. Bake in moderate oven, 350 degrees, for 1 hour. Uncover, and bake 30 to 45 minutes, or until tender.

Roast wild turkey, prepared properly, is always a treat.

## Turkey-Noodle Bake

Blend 1½ cups milk into a 10½-ounce can condensed cream of mushroom soup; stir in 3 beaten eggs. Add 3 ounces (about 2 cups) fine noodles, cooked and drained; 2 cups cubed cooked turkey; 1 cup soft bread crumbs (1½ slices); 4 ounces sharp processed American cheese, shredded, about 1 cup; ¼ cup chopped green pepper; ¼ cup butter or margarine, melted; and 2 tablespoons chopped canned pimiento. Turn into 13×9 baking dish.

Bake in moderate oven at 350 degrees for 30 to 40 minutes, or until knife inserted in center comes out clean. Cut in squares to serve.

## Ham-Turkey Pie

### Rice Shell
2½ cups cooked long-grain rice
2 beaten eggs
¼ cup butter or margarine, melted
⅛ teaspoon pepper

### Pie Filling
¼ cup butter or margarine
5 tablespoons all-purpose flour
¼ teaspoon pepper
2 cups chicken broth
1 cup chopped fully cooked ham
1 cup chopped cooked turkey

½ cup chopped mushrooms
¼ cup chopped green onion
3 tablespoons snipped parsley

To prepare rice shell, thoroughly combine cooked rice, beaten eggs, ¼ cup melted butter or margarine, and ⅛ teaspoon pepper. Press rice mixture firmly into an ungreased 9-inch pie plate. Set aside.

In a saucepan, melt remaining ¼ cup butter or margarine; blend in flour and ¼ teaspoon pepper. Add chicken broth all at once. Cook over medium heat, stirring constantly, until mixture thickens and bubbles. Remove from heat. Stir in chopped ham, chopped turkey, mushrooms, green onion and snipped parsley; mix thoroughly.

Pour ham-turkey mixture into prepared rice shell. Bake in a moderate oven at 350 degrees for 40 minutes. Let pie stand about 5 minutes before serving.

## Turkey Hash—Oven Style

1½ cups coarsely ground cooked turkey
1 cup cubed cooked potato
1 small can evaporated milk (⅔ cup)
¼ cup finely snipped parsley
¼ cup finely chopped onion
1 teaspoon Worcestershire sauce
½ teaspoon salt
¼ teaspoon ground sage
dash pepper

### Crumb Mixture:
¼ cup finely crushed saltine crackers (about 7 crackers)
1 tablespoon butter or margarine, melted

In a mixing bowl, stir together turkey, potato, evaporated milk, parsley, finely chopped onion, Worcestershire sauce, salt, sage and dash of pepper. Turn mixture into a greased 1-quart casserole.

Toss together saltine cracker crumbs and melted butter; sprinkle crumb mixture evenly over hash. Bake in a moderate oven at 350 degrees until heated through, about 30 minutes.

## Turkey-Tomato Bake

½ cup chopped onion
½ cup chopped celery
1 tablespoon butter or margarine
1 15-ounce can whole kernel corn, drained
1½ cups chopped cooked turkey
1 10¾-ounce can condensed tomato soup
⅓ cup catsup
1 ounce processed American cheese, shredded (¼ cup)
1 9-ounce package frozen French-fried crinkle-cut potatoes

In a skillet, cook onion and celery in butter until vegetables are tender but not brown. Stir in the corn, turkey, soup, catsup and cheese. Turn into an 8×8×2-inch baking dish. Arrange potatoes over top. Bake, uncovered, in a hot oven at 425 degrees for 25 minutes.

## Turkey Spoon Bread

½ cup chopped onion
¼ cup chopped green pepper
1 clove garlic, minced
1 tablespoon salad oil
1 15-ounce can tomato sauce
2 cups diced cooked turkey
1½ teaspoons chili powder
1 teaspoon sugar
½ teaspoon salt

Prepare spoon bread (see below). Cook onion, pepper and garlic in hot oil just until tender. Stir in remaining ingredients. Simmer, covered, 15 minutes. Serve over wedges of spoon bread.

### Spoon Bread

In a saucepan, gradually stir ⅔ cup yellow cornmeal into 2 cups milk, and cook until thickened. Add 1 cup shredded processed American cheese, 1 tablespoon butter, ¾ teaspoon baking powder, ½ teaspoon salt and ¼ teaspoon paprika. Stir until cheese melts. Gradually add a moderate amount of hot mixture to beaten egg yolks; beat well, and return to hot mixture. Beat 2 egg whites till stiff; fold into cornmeal mixture. Turn into greased 9-inch pie plate. Bake at 350 degrees for 40 to 45 minutes.

### Turkey Puff Casserole

    3 cups turkey stuffing
    2 to 3 cups sliced, cooked turkey
    1 tablespoon minced onion
    2 tablespoons butter
    2 tablespoons flour
    2 cups broth made from giblets
    ½ teaspoon ground ginger
    ½ teaspoon nutmeg
    salt and pepper
    2 beaten eggs
    2 tablespoons bread crumbs mixed
        in 1 tablespoon melted butter
    ½ teaspoon thyme

Grease 2½-quart casserole. Line bottom with a layer of stuffing. If packaged, mix according to instructions for 3 cups of dressing. Arrange slices of turkey in a layer over stuffing. Set aside and make sauce.

#### Sauce

Sauté onions in butter. Stir in flour, and gradually stir in broth and seasonings. Pour into beaten eggs, stirring well. Cool. Pour carefully into casserole and sprinkle with crumbs.

Place casserole in a pan of hot water and bake, uncovered, at 375 degrees for 45 minutes, until top is set. Can be cut in squares to serve on the plate, or served buffet style.

### Turkey Stew

    20-pound turkey
    6 pounds onion, diced
    6 pounds potatoes, diced
    1 No. 2 can corn
    1½ pounds fat back, diced
    1 bottle Worcestershire sauce
    1 quart tomato juice
    1½ jars mustard
    1½ pounds butter

Cook turkey in water until meat leaves the bone—about 3½ hours. Remove from water, and cut in bite-size pieces. Return to the turkey stock, add all other ingredients, and cook until vegetables are tender. Salt to taste.

### Leftover Turkey Terrapin

    2 cups turkey, cubed
    3 tablespoons margarine
    1½ tablespoons flour
    ¼ cup chicken broth (use bouillon cube)
    1½ cups heavy cream or evaporated milk
    8-ounce can sliced mushrooms
    2 hard-cooked eggs, chopped
    salt
    pepper
    paprika
    ¼-cup cooking sherry

Dust turkey with flour; lightly brown in melted margarine in large skillet. Blend in broth and add cream, mixing until smooth. Add mushrooms and eggs, and salt, paprika and pepper to taste. Heat thoroughly. Add cooking sherry. Serve on toast points or in pastry cups. Add pimiento if desired.

# 16

# Learning Aids

The quickest way to learn how to hunt turkeys is to employ a guide at a lodge on lands that have plenty of turkeys. Often novice hunters make the mistake of going to areas where few or no turkeys are available to hunt. To learn the sport, you must test your skills against the turkeys themselves. The more toms you encounter in a day of turkey hunting, the more opportunities you have to test the things you have learned. Also, when you hunt private lands, you will not have as much interference from other hunters as you will on public lands.

But to benefit from a guided hunt, you have to alter the usual routine. Most guides find the turkey for you and call the bird in to allow you to take the shot. Instead, talk to your guide before the hunt and tell him you are not nearly as interested in bagging a turkey as you are in learning how to hunt. Ask him to explain his choice of hunting area and why turkeys are there. As the hunt proceeds ask him to explain every move he makes and the behavior of the turkey. If he cooperates, you will learn more in three days than you can in a year or more of hunting on your own.

If you are not fortunate enough to hunt with a guide on private lands, you still can learn to hunt on public lands. Use this book as a guide.

However, anytime you can hunt with another, more experienced hunter, whether or not he is a guide, you will increase your knowledge of the sport. In twenty to forty days of hunting turkeys each season, I try to spend at least two-thirds of the mornings in the woods with other hunters. Although I have hunted turkeys for more than twenty years, everytime I hunt with another hunter I learn a new tactic, a different calling technique or a better way of moving through the woods. For me, turkey hunting is a continuing education. If you have the chance to hunt with someone with more experience than you, always seize that opportunity, and learn from other hunters. I do enjoy the solitude and the thrill of going one-on-one with gobblers, but I also have found the sport is far more fun for me when I share it with a friend.

Another way to learn how to hunt turkeys is to join your local chapter of the national Wild Turkey Federation (NWTF), an organization

**Teaming with an experienced turkey hunter not only increases your odds of taking a bird but is also the best way to learn the sport.**

of men who hunt the beards and spurs. At these meetings, the members share their hunting knowledge, make friends with each other and learn of opportunities to hunt with other sportsmen of like interests. Often you will meet the conservation officers of areas you want to hunt. They will know where to find land and turkeys to hunt, and they will introduce you to a knowledgeable turkey hunter who can teach you the sport.

Another productive way to learn the sport is to study turkey hunting videos. They show the elapsed time from when the hunter first hears the turkey gobble until he actually sees the bird or takes the shot. Study the video with a pencil in hand and make notes, especially about the elapsed time of each hunt. This is a good way to learn how long it takes to call in a gobbler. Then use these timetables as a rule of thumb when you hunt turkeys.

Turkey videos usually are made by master turkey hunters who know the importance of patience. Make note when you watch a turkey video of...

• The type of call he uses.
• How often he's calling.
• What type of terrain he's hunting.
• Where he takes a stand.
• How far he is from the turkey when he takes the shot.
• Why he takes the shot when he does.
• Why he misses the turkey, if he does miss.

• What he does immediately after the shot.

• How he carries the bird out of the woods.

If you cannot learn these things from the video, write the producer and ask him.

Another learning aid is a microcassette tape recorder and a sixty minute microcassette. Set the recorder at the slowest speed. Put it in a Zip-Loc plastic bag in your front pocket. As you hunt, record everything you learn on that tape recorder.

• What time of morning you hear the first turkey gobble.

• Where you are when you hear the turkey gobble and from which compass direction the sound comes.

• The direction of the road or path you are on when you hear the turkey.

• Whether the turkey is gobbling aggressively or very little. Then you will know how to call to the gobbler once you get close to him.

• What the various terrain breaks are that you cross as you approach the turkey. Did you cross planted pines, hardwood timber and/or a mountain? Was there thick cover between you and the turkey? This information is important if you ever return to hunt the same area.

• What type of area you set up in to call the turkey.

• How quickly the turkey answers you.

• How much time elapses between your first call and the appearance of the turkey.

• When you take the shot.

• Which direction the bird flies if you miss him.

This information is important to the success of your next hunt. Turkeys have a very definite

**Record valuable hunting information on a microcassette that you carry on the hunt.**

pecking order. When one tom is bagged in an area, another moves up in the pecking order. Often this bird will travel the same route, roost in a tree in the same region and meet his hens in the same spot. By recording your hunt, you prepare yourself for another hunt in the same area.

Learning better ways to find and call turkeys, and then outsmart them, is more enjoyable than squeezing the trigger. That is the ultimate challenge of the sport.

# Glossary

**BEARD:** A hairlike growth that protrudes from a turkey's chest. Both male and female turkeys can have beards, but the beard is the primary sexual characteristic of the male. Beards generally grow at a rate of four to five inches a year. Growth begins when turkeys are about five months old.

**BOX CALLER:** A thin-walled box with a wooden paddle lid attached to one end. With this box, most all turkey calls can be imitated. To create the friction-based sounds, the lid and two sides of the box are usually chalked.

**CACKLING:** An excited call given by the hen turkey and made up of a series of fast yelps.

**CALLING:** Sounds made by the hunter to lure a gobbler into gun range. Calling is not limited to the use of hen or gobbler voice imitations. To mimic other sounds made by turkeys, many hunters scratch in the leaves, beat a turkey wing against tree limbs and bushes or slap the sides of their legs with their gloved hands.
*Sweet Calling:* Any turkey voice imitation performed with a smooth, clear, crisp tone.
*Raspy Calling:* A call made by a hen that sounds as though she has a sore throat or the beginnings of laryngitis.

**CALL-LESS HUNTING:** Attempting to bag a turkey without calling to him. To be a productive call-less hunter, you must know where and when you can meet a tom in the woods during his daily routine. This type of hunting requires much more knowledge of the turkeys, their movement patterns, and their likes and dislikes than does hunting with a call.

**CALL-SHY:** A term describing a turkey that will not come to conventional calling. Often this bird has been called to by hunters and perhaps shot at and spooked. A call-shy gobbler may not come to a hen but will gobble and wait for her to come to him, as she's naturally supposed to do. If he gobbles and she does not come, some hunters think he will walk off because he assumes the calling is coming from a hunter.

**CARUNCLE:** Small, fleshy, reddish growths of skin at the base of the turkey's throat.

**CEDAR BOX WITH STRIKER:** A cedar box caller is similar to the box and paddle box caller with which most hunters are familiar. However, instead of a paddle for the lid of the box caller, the hunter has some type of striker he holds in his hand and freely passes across the lid to produce the calls of a wild gobbler.

**CLUCK:** A hen turkey's sound that is much like a woman talking to herself.

*Contented Cluck:* The sound a hen turkey makes while walking through the woods when everything is great in her world.

*Excited Cluck:* A hen turkey's sound that can mean, "I think there's something over there we'd better look at. Hang on, I'm on the way."

**CONTROLLED BURNING:** The act of setting fire to the woods to burn away the litter on the ground. The fire releases nutrients into the soil and causes a new growth of young plants without damaging or destroying the timber. Controlled burning is a key management tool for improving turkey habitat.

**CROW CALL:** The sounds that crows make when they notify one another of their positions. The crow call is used by turkey hunters to cause a tom to gobble instinctively. Many times when a turkey hears a high-pitched noise like a crow call, he reacts as you do when someone jumps out of a dark closet and shots, "Boo!" You may scream, because that is the first vocalization that you give to the emotion you feel when you're frightened unexpectedly.

**CUTTING:** Very fast, loud stutter yelps and clucks, made by a hen, much like the beginning of a cackle, but not going all the way through a cackle. Cutting often means, "If you're looking for a date, I'm the lady who can satisfy."

**DECOY:** An artificial reproduction of a hen turkey. Many hunters use a mounted hen or a plastic replica as a decoy. Some tough gobblers will come in to a hunter only if they see as well as hear what they perceive to be a hen.

**DIAPHRAGM CALLER:** A caller made of tape, lead, and latex rubber that is inserted into the roof of the hunter's mouth. When air passes over the rubber diaphragm, the hunter can make many of the calls of the hen turkey and the gobbler.

**DISPLAYING:** The strutting of a gobbler.

**DOMINANT GOBBLER:** The gobbler whose strength, size, age and intelligence put him at the top of the pecking order in a flock. Sometimes called a boss gobbler. Many times a dominant gobbler will keep subdominant toms from gobbling. He claims the right to breed the hens because of his superiority.

**DOMINANT HEN:** The female boss of a flock. Often the dominant hen determines which way a flock will travel, and she is generally the one that calls a scattered flock back together.

**DOUBLE CALLING:** Calling done by two hunters at the same time, to imitate a number of turkeys in the same area.

**DROPPINGS:** Turkey excretion in a stool form. A gobbler dropping has the shape of a fishhook or question mark. A hen's stool is round and resembles a small cow dropping.

**DRUMMING:** The sound a tom turkey makes when he struts. This sounds much like the shifting of gears of an 18-wheel tractor-trailer truck.

**EASTERN WILD TURKEY** (*Meleagris gallopavo silvestris*): One of the subspecies of the North American wild turkey found mainly in the eastern United States.

**FLY-UP/FLY-DOWN CACKLE:** An excited call the hen turkey makes when she jumps off a limb in the morning and flies down to the ground to greet a new day, or when she jumps off the ground to fly into a tree for a night's rest. The cackle usually begins with a series of excited clucks, followed by a series of fast yelps.

**FRICTION CALL:** Any type of call consisting of two objects rubbed together to produce the sounds that turkeys make. A slate and peg, a box call, or a Twin Hen (a call made of aluminum and wood with a peg striker) are all examples of friction callers.

**GOBBLE:** The sound made by a tom that gives away his location, calls hens to mate and notifies other turkeys he is in the area.

**GOBBLER:** A male turkey.

**GOULD TURKEY** (*Meleagris gallopavo mexicano*): A turkey once found in Arizona and New Mexico as well as Mexico that biologists have been helping to make a comeback.

**HAWK CALL:** The sound a hawk makes as it flies overhead. This is the same call turkey hunters use to cause turkeys to shock-gobble.

**HEN:** A female turkey.

**HUNG-UP:** What happens when a turkey stops just out of gun range and refuses to come closer to the hunter.

**IMPRINT:** The process by which baby turkey poults at birth immediately follow their mother and learn to do as she does.

**INTERGRADE:** A turkey produced by the interbreeding of two different turkey subspecies. Intergrades of the eastern turkey and the Florida turkey are common in a narrow zone across the South.

**JAKE:** A one-year-old gobbler.

**KEE-KEE RUN:** A young gobbler's squeal and call. This is the call most often given by young gobblers before they learn how to gobble and the call that turkey hunters imitate mostly in the fall, though sometimes in the spring. In the fall, the jakes (one-year-old gobblers) have not matured enough to be able to gobble. So their sound resembles, *Peep, peep, peep, yelp, yelp, yelp,* which is the *kee-kee* run.

**LONGBEARD:** A dominant or boss gobbler, usually more than two years old.

**LOST CALL:** A call given by hunters to pull a turkey flock together or to locate a gobbler. Another name for the lost call is the assembly call.

**MERRIAM TURKEY** (*Meleagris gallopavo merriami*): One of the subspecies of North American wild turkey found in the western United States.

**MEXICAN TURKEY** (*Meleagris gallopavo gallopavo*): One of six subspecies of North American wild turkey, now extinct, that was originally located in the central part of Mexico and is the forefather of the domestic turkey.

**MOUTH YELPER:** A diaphragm caller.

**OCELLATED TURKEY** (*Meleagris ocellata*) One of two species of turkeys, the other being the North American wild turkey, *Meleagris gallopavo*. Having some blue coloration, the ocellated turkey is found in the Yucatan of Mexico and nearby central American states, and is considered to be by many the loveliest wild turkey.

**OSCEOLA TURKEY** (*Meleagris gallopavo osceola*): The Florida turkey, which lives only in the Sunshine State, primarily in the southern part of the state, is named for the Seminole Indian chief Osceola.

**OWL HOOTER:** A caller that reproduces the voice of the barred owl. The owl hooter is used to locate turkeys, which will shock-gobble in response.

**OWLING:** Hunter calls that imitate the sound of an owl.

**PATTERN BOARD:** A sheet of plywood or metal that catches the shot from a discharged shotgun shell. On the pattern board, the hunter can see the density and size of the pattern of shot expended from his shell. Shooting at a pattern board tells him how effective his shotgun will be at various ranges with different loads.

**PECKING ORDER:** The social hierarchy of the turkey flock; the order of dominance of the individual turkeys within a flock.

**PEG:** A wooden stick or a round piece of plastic that is stroked across a slate box, a piece of slate, or an aluminum-covered box to imitate the sound of a turkey. The peg is a part of a friction call.

**PIPPING:** Short, high-pitched tones the mother hen makes to encourage her poults to break out of their eggs while they are in the nest. Soon the poults in the eggs make their own pipping noises as they imitate their mother.

**POULT:** A baby turkey.

**PREDATOR:** An animal that feeds on other animals. Some of the predators of turkeys include wild dogs, bobcats, foxes, raccoons, eagles, coyotes, wolves, crows, skunks, and snakes.

**PURR:** A contented sound made by a hen, much like a woman's humming.

**PUSH-BUTTON CALL:** A simple friction call that requires the hunter only to push a peg with his finger to produce hen calls.

**PUTT:** An alarm sound given by a turkey.

**RIO GRANDE TURKEY** (*Meleagris gallopavo intermedia*): A turkey in the western U.S. Usually is larger in weight than most other North American turkeys.

**ROOST:** A particular tree where a turkey perches during the night for sleeping.

**SCOUTING:** Taking inventory of the area you plan to hunt. Looking for turkey sign, listening for turkey sounds, and becoming aware of the terrain and habitat can help in determining a hunt plan.

**SET-UP:** The place where you take a stand to call a turkey. A good set-up will generally be in clean woods with no natural barriers the turkey must cross to get to you.

**SHOCK GOBBLE:** The instinctive reaction of a turkey in response to some type of loud sound. A tom may shock-gobble when he hears a car door slamming, a train whistle, a clap of thunder, a crow call, or any other loud, high-pitched noise.

**SLATE CALL:** A caller consisting of a peg and a piece of slate. The peg is stroked across the slate to produce the sound of the turkey. The slate is sometimes enclosed in plastic, wood or even a turtle shell.

**SNOOD, SNOOT OR DEWBILL:** A bump on the forehead of a turkey that changes size according to how excited the turkey is.

**SNUFF BOX:** A caller made from a snuff can. The bottom and half of the top are cut away, and latex rubber is stretched over part of the open half of the top. To operate the snuff box caller, the hunter rests his bottom lip against the rubber and blows air across it. The sound made from the air rushing across the rubber is amplified within the snuff can. The snuff box was the forerunner of what is commonly known today as the tube caller.

**SPUR:** A horny growth on a male turkey's leg, which sometimes also occurs on a hen's leg. At two years of age, most gobblers have one one-inch spur on each leg. However, some gobblers have no spurs, and some have multiple spurs.

**STRIKER BOX:** Either a slate-covered or an aluminum-covered wooden box used by rubbing a wooden peg across it to imitate the call of a wild turkey. This type of caller is also known as a friction call.

**STRUTTING:** The action seen when a turkey coils his neck, flares his feathers, spreads his tail, and drops his wings to impress a hen. A strutting turkey is much like a man on the beach who flexes his muscles to draw attention to himself and impress the ladies.

**STRUT ZONE:** An area where a turkey goes on a regular basis to strut and meet a hen for breeding.

**SUBDOMINANT GOBBLERS AND HENS:** Turkeys subservient to the dominant birds in a flock. A subdominant turkey may become dominant if the dominant turkey is removed from the flock.

**TIGHT PATTERN:** A shot pattern in which the pellets are close together at the point on the target where the hunter is aiming. A tight pattern is much more effective for turkey hunting than a loose pattern.

**TRAVELING TURKEY:** A gobbler that will answer a call but moves farther away from the call each time he hears it.

**TREADING NOTE:** A call known today as a cackle.

**TREE CALL OR TREE YELP:** A very soft series of yelps given by a hen before she flies down from her roost. The tree yelp may be best described as a quiet yawn.

**TUBE CALLER:** A caller made of plastic and resembling a miniature megaphone. The tube caller has a piece of latex rubber over its end that the hunter blows against to make the sounds of the turkey. The tube caller is the modern descendant of the snuff-box caller.

**TURKEY MANAGEMENT:** The manipulation of habitat, predators, turkeys, and hunters to produce the optimum number of turkeys on a given piece of land.

**TURKEY SIGN:** Anything left on the ground that indicates that a turkey is in the area. Signs include droppings, feathers, scratches, dusting areas and tracks.

**WATTLES:** The fatty tissue around a turkey's neck.

**WING-BONE CALLER:** A caller made from a turkey's wing bone. The hunter sucks air through the bone to make the sound of a wild turkey. There are also artificial wing-bone callers that resemble pipes.

**YELP:** A call that varies in rhythm from turkey to turkey.
*Contented Yelp:* A call a hen gives when she is walking through the woods with nothing in particular on her mind.
*Excited Yelp:* A call a hen gives when she is either frightened, looking forward to meeting her gobbler or excited for some other reason.
*Prospecting Yelp:* A call that says, "I'm over here. Is there anyone out there to talk to?"

# Map Sources

Maps are available to help you to find places to hunt and camp. Here is a list of map sources.

**U. S. Geological Survey**
**Federal Center, Building 41**
**P. O. Box 25286**
**Denver, Colorado 80225**

Purchase indexes and order forms for the maps of states west of the Mississippi River, including Alaska and Hawaii, from this address. The U. S. Geological Survey, which has mapped the entire United States, has topographical maps to scale available at $2.50 each that contain line and symbol representations of natural terrain and manmade structures. These maps will aid a hunter in determining where roads, rivers, firebreaks and property lines are on a specific piece of property. Most outdoorsmen prefer the 22" × 27" maps, which depict on a large scale the amount of land a hunter usually can walk in a day.

The indexes of the topographical maps name the region covered by each map, the scale available and the year the area was surveyed. These indexes also include lists of special maps that have been made of a place as well as the names and addresses of map dealers, map reference libraries and federal distribution centers.

"Topographical Map Symbols," "Topographical Maps: Silent Guides for the Outdoorsman" and "Maps for America: Cartographic Products of the U. S. Geological Survey and Others" are pamphlets available from either of the U. S. Geological Survey centers that help explain the various kinds of maps as well as the meanings of the symbols, lines, etc., on the maps.

**U. S. Geological Survey**
**1200 South Eads Street**
**Arlington, VA 22202**

Write to this address to order topographical maps for states east of the Mississippi River.

Many libraries have sets of topographical maps available as well as order forms and indexes for the maps. Also the library near the place where you plan to hunt may contain maps of that county that are not accessible in other parts of the state.

**Division of Wildlife Refuges**
**U. S. Fish and Wildlife Service**
**Department of the Interior**
**Room 2343**

Washington, D. C. 20402

This department distributes free maps of the more than 400 wildlife refuges under federal protection.

**National Wetlands Inventory Office**
**U. S. Fish and Wildlife Service**
**Department of the Interior**
**Washington, D. C. 20204**

Approximately 10,000 acres of wetlands are mapped by this group.

**Water and Power Resources Service**
**Office of Public Affairs**
**Department of the Interior**
**Washington, D. C. 20240**

Write for free recreation maps of the facilities of this group, formerly the Bureau of Reclamation, across the United States at 333 reservoirs, including camping areas, etc.

**"Field Offices of the Forest Service"**
**Office of Public Affairs**
**Forest Service**
**Department of Agriculture**
**South Building, Room 3008**
**Washington, D. C. 20250**

This free pamphlet lists the locations and addresses of all national forests and grasslands. Write the National Forest Service office nearest you to order maps of any of the 122 national forests, and indicate what types of activities you are planning, since the Forest Service sometimes produces different maps for hikers, hunters, campers, etc. The maps generally cost $1–$2 each.

**U. S. Government Printing Office**
**Superintendent of Documents**
**Washington, D. C. 20402**

By writing the above address or visiting the GPO nearest you, you can find many helpful pamphlets and maps.

"National Parks of the U. S.—Guide and Map" is a map available that shows the locations of the national parks and includes a chart listing the services, facilities and activities in each park.

"Maps and Atlases—SB-102" and "Surveying and Mapping—SB-183" are two subject bibliographies available free from the GPO too.

**U. S. Army Corps of Engineers**
**Office of Public Affairs**
**Department of the Army**
**2 Massachusetts Avenue, N. W.**
**Washington, D. C. 20314**

The Corps of Engineers produces and distributes maps of the recreation areas it manages, but each map must be ordered from the district where the recreational area is located. By writing the above address, you can learn the Corps' districts and addresses.

**Office of Public Affairs**
**Federal Energy Regulatory Commission**
**825 North Capital Street, N. E.**
**Washington, D. C. 20426**

This commission can give you information about various maps available on the hydroelectric projects licensed by the U. S. Department of Energy where there are public facilities for hunting, camping and other activities.

**National Cartographic Information Center**
**507 National Center**
**12201 Sunrise Valley Drive**
or
**345 Middlefield Road**
**Menlo Park, CA 94025**

This center is the part of the U. S. Geological Survey that is the main source for maps that are produced or distributed by federal agencies, as well as by commercial publishers. Some of the free publications include, "Types of Maps Published by Government Agencies," "Finding Your Way With Map and Compass," and "Popular Publications of the U.S. Geological Survey."

**Defense Mapping Agency**
**Office of Distribution Services**
**Department of the Army**
**Attention: DDCP**
**Washington, D. C. 20315**
Write this source for information on topographical maps of the U. S. as contained in the "Catalog of Maps, Charts and Related Products."

**Bureau of Land Management.** Learn the addresses of the BLM offices nearest to the land you plan to hunt by visiting your library and studying the *United States Government Organization Manual.* The BLM offers access to some fine outdoor recreation in the western states and has a series of 60-minute quadrangle maps at a cost of $4 each that show land contours, roads, streams, lakes and manmade structures along with color codings to indicate whether the owner of the land is federal, state, private, etc.

**Federal Depository Libraries**
**Consumer Information Center**
**Pueblo, CO 81009**
By contacting this center, you can receive a list of the public, college and government libraries throughout the U. S. that receive copies of most federal government publications, including maps.
Large landholding companies in areas you plan to hunt, including timber companies, steel corporations, mining concerns and power companies will have maps available to show where permit hunting can be done.

**Florida Game and Fish Commission**
**620 South Meridian Street**
**Tallahassee, Fl 32399-1600**
**PH: (904) 488-1960**
*(For information about public hunting lands for Osceolas)*

**National Wild Turkey Federation**
**770 Augusta Road**
**POB 530**
**Edgefield, SC 29824-0530**
**PH: (803) 637-3106**
*(For information on managing turkeys)*

**San Angelo Company, Inc.**
**P.O. Box 984**
**San Angelo, TX 76902**
*(For skullcaps to use on turkey mounts)*

**Touchstone Taxidermy Supply**
**Rt. 1, Box 5294**
**Bossier City, LA 71111**
*(For Instant Mounting Fluid to use in preserving a turkey)*